AGGRESSORS

VOLUME 3

INTERCEPTOR VS. HEAVY BOMBER

Text by DAVID A. ANDERTON
Illustrations by RIKYU WATANABE

Airlife
England

Above: Boeing B-17G Flying Fortresses of the 452nd BG, 8th AF. (USAF)
Below: Messerschmitt Bf109G-6/R3/R6 of 3/JG 27. (Bundesarchiv)

Background photograph: Searchlights over a German city. (Bundesarchiv)
Inset: A night fighter pilot in Messerschmitt Bf110D. (Bundesarchiv)

Copyright © 1991 by Zokeisha Publications Ltd., Tokyo/New York. All rights reserved.
Edited by Yoji Watanabe.

This edition first published in the UK in 1991
by Airlife Publishing Ltd.

British Library Cataloguing in Publication Data available

ISBN 1 85310 241 5

Understanding Interception

The dark hulk moved in a straight line, steady and unsuspecting, toward a distant point on the land. More than an hour earlier it had begun this journey, with other black shapes, streaming out of the evening mist in loose formation.

Behind and well off to the side, the hunters kept pace. All their sensors were alert, observing the flowing river of somber shapes, narrowing their choice to a few that seemed to be straggling, unable to match the pace of the main body.

Then, the specific target selected, the hunters began to close in, moving faster, angling toward the steadily moving dark bodies. Two hunters gained speed, gauging their run-in to end at a point where their victim soon would be. The other hunters accelerated to keep up, remaining on tracks parallel to the stream.

Then the paired hunters and their victim were at almost the same place at the same time. The hunters struck, swiftly and savagely. Their leonine claws and teeth grasped and held the wildebeest; their attack brought him to the ground. In moments, the animal was dead, and the victorious lions were calling in the rest of the pride to share the kill.

Lions on the attack are a cruelly beautiful example of effective interception tactics. They first detect their victims, scenting them, seeing them, hearing their movements. Then they observe, watching for young, old, and infirm animals, or stragglers. The hunters split into tactical units, one or two lions to a team. While the killing team begins its interception, the other lions stay at the periphery of the herd, ready to move it to the advantage of the hunters, or to confine it to a killing ground.

Watch the chase. The hunters move instinctively, speeding to an intercept point where the wildebeest will be. Older and wiser lions know that a tail chase will be fruitless, most of the time; younger ones have to learn that through experience. The hunters slash through the herd, eyes fixed on their quarry, and attack from the rear quarters, leaping on the wildebeest to bring it down, then biting its throat to suffocate it.

Their intercept is most effective when they work as a team, hunters and killers with a single goal, and the knowledge that a kill is a shared prize.

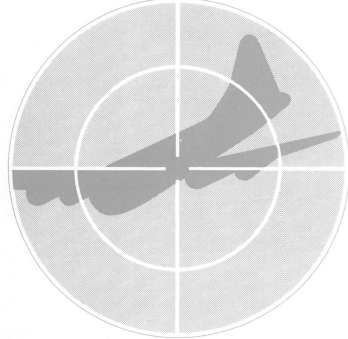

The emblem of IV (*Sturm*)/JG3

Early man learned killing tactics by watching predators. He learned the importance of team efforts, of early detection, of trying to direct the quarry into a killing ground. Bred into countless generations of increasingly intelligent humans, the basic tactics of interception seem now to be one of our instincts.

A duck hunter hears the ducks calling, watches the skies, sees the flock, selects his target, and brings down his quarry with a single shot. In his mind, the hunter performed a complex computation of the equations of motion of two moving bodies: the duck, and a grouping of pellets. That also is interception.

In this book, we discuss the tactics of interception used, specifically, to attack heavy bombers during World War II, providing sufficient historical background to add depth to understanding.

The word, "interception," is derived from Latin: *inter* (between) and *capere* (to seize). It is the seizing or stopping on the way, or the preventing of someone or something from reaching a destination, the action described in Western movies: "Let's head 'em off at the pass!"

One of the best and earliest descriptions of aircraft interception principles was written in clear and simple language, and then taught to pilots of the U.S. Army Air Corps by Capt. Claire L. Chennault. His classroom was the Air Corps Tactical School, Maxwell Field, Alabama.

Chennault had the bad luck to be in a hotbed of tactics development that was either geared to bombardment or to the established (and outmoded) practices over the Western Front during World War I. Official Air Corps doctrines were coalescing around the long-range bomber, and one widely held belief was that a determined bomber force would always get through to the target. Chennault disagreed, frequently and with acerbity. His argument was that pursuits could stop bombers, or at least hurt them so badly that it would be equal to stopping them. Because Chennault's arguments went against official truths, his reputation and later career suffered.

The standard Air Corps pursuit tactics of the time, specifically those taught at the Tactical School, were leftovers from World War I. The chief instructors were men who had helped forge the fledgling air weapons of that time, and who were convinced that the useful tactics of 1918 would remain useful into the foreseeable future. Pursuits flew on patrols, swept assigned sectors, and kept a lookout for enemy aircraft of any type. When they saw an enemy, pilots positioned themselves with the sun at their backs, if possible. They attacked in a diving assault, and each singled out an enemy to fight one-on-one in the classic dogfight of the skies above the fields of France.

Chennault wrote a simple and short text, "The Role of Defensive Pursuit," had it mimeographed, and distributed it to his students at the Tactical School. It stated that successful air defense has three phases: (1) detect and report the strength and direction of the enemy attack force; (2) intercept that force with suitably sized elements of pursuit aircraft; and (3) destroy or repulse the attackers.

Basically, that description could have been applied to existing tactics. But Chennault was against standing patrols; he believed it was more effective to dispatch a force after the enemy strength and direction of attack had been determined. It would save fuel, guarantee the enemy would be met, and would

Curtiss Hawk 81A-2 (P-40B) of AVG at airfield in Burma in early 1942. (Imperial War Museum)

dispatch only the necessary number of fighters to do the job, instead of maintaining large airborne forces.

Chennault recommended establishing a ground network of reporting stations, connected by telephone lines to a central operation headquarters. The network might be augmented by airborne picket aircraft. Attacking bombers were to be tracked continuously from first detection until they disappeared on their way back to base. Pursuit aircraft wait on alert, but on the ground; the operations center determines the best point and time of intercept, and then scrambles the fighters. On their way to the targets, they receive, by radio, any further data required to intercept.

In an interesting aside, Chennault suggested that light bombs, dropped from above by pursuits, would be effective against heavy bombers by scattering their formations to reduce their collective firepower. U.S. air tacticians never approved that, although it is probable that some U.S. pilots, at some time, tried it. But both German and Japanese interceptor pilots used the tactic extensively during World War II, and with some effectiveness.

After Chennault had retired for medical reasons and the knowledge that his USAAC career was at a dead end, he finally got the chance to practice what he had preached. Invited to China in 1937 to inspect the country's air units, he stayed to train Chinese airmen and to organize an early warning network that became the prototype of later interceptor systems. It began with a telephone and telegraph network connecting Nanking, the Chinese capital, with Shanghai and Hangchow, the major military airbases. Added to that network was a force of interceptors, held on the ground until the correct moment.

Before then, Japanese bombers controlled the air over China. They bombed with impunity and machine-gunned from lower altitudes with little or no opposition. Chennault's tactical interception system threatened them. The embattled Japanese bomber forces sent a desperate call for help, asking that escort fighters be sent to safeguard their bombers. The arrival of Mitsubishi A6M2 Zero fighters turned the tide temporarily.

Next, Chennault replaced his force of biplanes with new Curtiss P-40B fighters, flown by volunteers—mercenaries,

more accurately—drawn from adventurous and disaffected pilots of U.S. Army, Navy and Marine Corps air units. The American Volunteer Group (later nicknamed "The Flying Tigers") was trained and retrained by Chennault in the tactics of efficient interception. After their first learning experiences in combat, they began a long campaign that eventually turned back the Japanese tide in the air. By the time the AVG was absorbed into the China Air Task Force in July 1942, its pilots had claimed 299 Japanese aircraft destroyed in the air, 153 possibly destroyed, and more that 200 destroyed on the ground. AVG recorded losses were 23 pilots killed in action or in accidents, 12 P-40s lost in combat, and 61 aircraft destroyed in accidents.

Not all of these victory claims were the result of interceptions; but the one-sided score was a testament to the training in basic tactics absorbed by the AVG pilots. And for those who rightly question the reported statistics, consider two points. First, the AVG action definitely rebuffed the Japanese aerial armadas and defeated them in the air, regardless of the final victory scores. Second, even if the AVG claims were inflated by a factor of ten—and most claims made under combat conditions need tempering by a deflation factor of perhaps two or three—they still outgunned the Japanese by a substantial margin.

And so we come to the eve of World War II and a look at the concepts developed during that conflict to destroy or turn back bombers. During those years of battle between September 1939 and August 1945, interception tactics and weapons bridged the time gap between World War I and contemporary conflict.

At the start of the war, interception tactics were closely related to those developed over the Western Front between 1914 and 1918. By the end of the war, there was more than a hint of the future direction of the battle between heavy bombers and interceptors. Jet-powered interceptors crammed with radar, armed with large-caliber automatic cannon, and directed effectively from the ground had appeared in combat units at squadron strength. And unmanned missiles, guided to the intercept by radar, perhaps carrying acoustic and infrared sensors, were in high-priority development and test programs.

Evolution of Interception Tactics

The pioneering American aviator Glenn Curtiss wrote in 1910: "It would be perfectly practical to drop enough dynamite…on…a city like New York to destroy it utterly." On June 30, 1911, Curtiss "bombed" a buoy-marked target defining a simulated battleship deck. His weapons: eight-inch (20 cm) lengths of lead pipe; he dropped 17, scoring 15 hits.

In Libya, the next year, Italian airmen dropped homemade bombs on rebellious Bedouin tribesmen. From then on, bombing as a tactic, and bombers as specialized military aircraft, began to gain supporters among airmen who looked toward the future.

In August 1914, German armies were on the road to Paris, and Belgians were struggling to hold Antwerp. In the sky over that beleaguered city loomed the menacing bulk of the German Zeppelin *Sachsen*; it showered down a ton of tiny bombs, bursting on impact to send shrapnel flying. That attack was the initial impetus of the Zeppelin menace that was to pose a fearsome threat to civilian populations and military concentrations.

Retaliation came soon. Daring airmen from Britain's Royal Naval Air Service flew their frail biplanes off forward bases in Antwerp on October 8, nursed them across the border to Germany, and bombed the railroad station in Cologne and the Zeppelin shed at Düsseldorf. The Zeppelin Z.9, new and untried in combat, went up in flames.

Escalation followed. A German Friedrichshafen FF29 biplane on floats, assigned to the German Navy's *See Flieger Abteilung* 1 (Ocean Fliers Division One) at Zeebrugge, left its base December 21, put-putted serenely across the Channel to Dover, dropped a pair of bombs in the Straits, and went home. No casualties, no damage, no intercepts.

But the threat of Zeppelin attack had spurred a reaction. Whatever aircraft the British could assemble—including, curiously, a German Albatross D.II—had been designated as defenders of the realm and assigned to airfields lying between the Channel and London, the obvious target. Further Zeppelin attacks were delayed, and the crew of the FF29 tried again. On Christmas Day 1914, they flew up the Thames toward London.

The British were ready. Up from the company aerodrome at Joyce Green buzzed a Vickers F.B.5 (Fighting Biplane 5, commonly called a "Gunbus") from No. 7 Squadron, Royal Flying Corps, piloted by 2nd Lt. Montagu R. Chidson with Cpl. Martin as his observer/gunner. They intercepted the FF29 at 1:15 p.m. at about 4,000 ft (1,220 m) over Erith, a dozen or so miles down the Thames from London's center. The German crew saw the oncoming Gunbus and swung around to retreat back down the river. The pursuit proceeded over Purfleet and Tilbury; the FF29 bombed a field near Cliffe.

Cpl. Martin's Lewis machine gun jammed and the F.B.5's Gnome engine was running rough, so Chidson abandoned the chase to land at Eastchurch at 2:00 p.m. The crew had been in the air since 12:35 p.m., had successfully completed the first aerial interception of an attacking bomber, and had driven it off.

It's not generally realized that there was a "Battle of Britain" during World War I. German Zeppelins and heavy bombers mounted strike after strike against the island, killing civilians and destroying houses. Those were the first of the terror raids, designed to break civilian morale. Like their successors, they failed utterly in that objective.

Also like their successors, they prodded military leadership into the development of a countermeasure, an integrated system of interception. Before World War I ended, the British had developed and put in place all its basic elements. It had an early warning network, with acoustic detectors, searchlights, and observers. It used anti-aircraft artillery, barrage balloons, and searchlights to channel incoming bomber attacks into aerial killing grounds. It employed the most modern fighters, operating from a chain of bases that lay along the Channel and North Sea coasts of England and extended in depth to protect London. It used primitive aircraft radios for ground control of the intercepts.

Weapons experts developed, in parallel, a panoply of weaponry that began with light Lewis and Vickers machine guns and small bombs. It included hand-held .45-caliber (11.4 mm) Martini-Henry carbines firing incendiary bullets; Hale rifle grenades; ten and 20 lb (4.5 and 9 kg) bombs; 3/4 and two U.S. gal (2.8 and 7.6 ltr) tin-and-copper canister gasoline bombs. The fearsome Farnborough Fiery Grapnel was a large fishhook to be

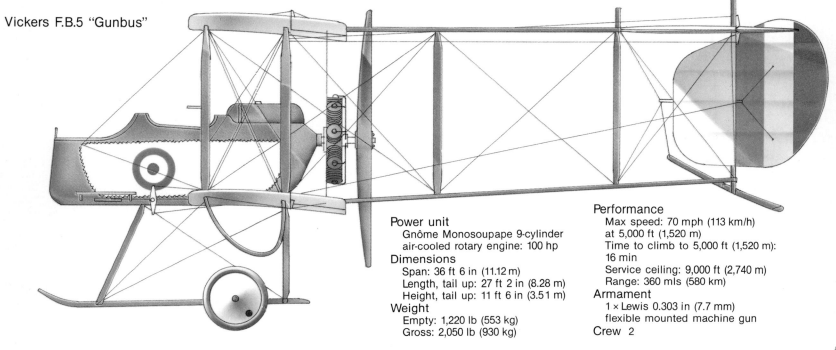

Vickers F.B.5 "Gunbus"

Power unit
Gnôme Monosoupape 9-cylinder air-cooled rotary engine: 100 hp

Dimensions
Span: 36 ft 6 in (11.12 m)
Length, tail up: 27 ft 2 in (8.28 m)
Height, tail up: 11 ft 6 in (3.51 m)

Weight
Empty: 1,220 lb (553 kg)
Gross: 2,050 lb (930 kg)

Performance
Max speed: 70 mph (113 km/h) at 5,000 ft (1,520 m)
Time to climb to 5,000 ft (1,520 m): 16 min
Service ceiling: 9,000 ft (2,740 m)
Range: 360 mls (580 km)

Armament
1 × Lewis 0.303 in (7.7 mm) flexible mounted machine gun

Crew 2

lowered on a cable to snag a Zeppelin. Then an explosive charge slid down the cable and detonated (wisely, this device never was used in combat). If all else failed, British pilots were instructed to ram the Zeppelin.

The early use of aircraft above the battlefields of World War I spurred its proponents into developing further concepts of air power after that war. World powers began to accept the need for air arms with varying degrees of enthusiasm. The *Luftwaffe* began its secret rebuilding, first in Russia, and then openly. The Italians took their force to reclaim ancient Rome's North African Empire. Britain and France built fleets of interceptors and defensive fighters. The USSR built attackers to assist and support its infantry and armor.

Only in the U.S., and there only in the face of great difficulties, did the concept of the heavy bomber become the strategic sword of air power. In every other country, the bomber was a tactical weapon, confined by reasons of roles, missions, and geography to a supporting role. In the United States, the prophets of air power saw the bomber as the Queen of the Skies, the battleship of the cloudless aerial ocean.

An interesting point: almost all countries made major efforts to produce light or medium fast bombers. Twin-engined, lightly armed, they were regarded as able to strike but invulnerable to being struck. Time and again, press stories of the period refer to new bombers that could outrun the fleetest fighters. The wish became accepted as fact, although it never was except under special circumstances.

When Germany went to war in September 1939, its military commanders had accepted the belief that it would be a short, sharp war, a true "*Blitzkrieg*." In such a war, tactical actions would predominate, and there would be no need for a strategic air arm of heavy bombers. Instead, the air arm would provide tactical support for the ground forces, armor,

Vickers Wellington Mk Is of No. 9 Squadron. Some bombers of the squadron were shot down on December 18, 1939. (Imperial War Museum)

and mobile infantry units. Further, because the prospective enemies of Germany—Poland, France, the Low Countries, England—had no existing heavy bomber fleets, and not much strength in the bomber squadrons they did have, the Germans believed the *Luftwaffe* could get along without home-defense fighters. The air defense of the Third Reich was assigned to anti-aircraft artillery units, augmented at night by searchlight batteries.

But the German Navy, concerned about possible strikes against its coastal installations, sponsored development and production of the FuMG 80 *Freya* radar, a mobile, motorized unit for search and for fighter ground control. It operated on a 2.4 m (7 ft $10\frac{1}{2}$ in) wavelength and could detect bomber-sized

Messerschmitt Bf110Cs of I/ZG 76 on the snowy airfield at Jever in the winter of 1939–40. Sixteen Bf110s of this Gruppe took part in the fighting against RAF Wellingtons over the north coast of Germany on December 18, 1939. (Bundesarchiv)

targets at a distance of about 100 km (62 mls) and altitudes above 3,000 m (9,840 ft).

Wilhelmshaven was a major German seaport and home port for North Sea Fleet battleships. The British scheduled the third RAF heavy bomber raid of the war against that harbor during daylight, December 18, 1939. The assigned force: two dozen Vickers Wellingtons, backbone of Bomber Command. They carried a maximum bomb load of about 4,500 lb (2,040 kg). Officially classed as medium bombers, they were then the heaviest bombers in European skies. For the raid, their weapon load was 500 lb (227 kg) semi-armor piercing bombs.

An experimental *Freya* radar unit, attached to a *Luftwaffe* signals batallion, had been stationed near Wilhelmshaven for operational trials. Its crew detected a bomber formation approaching and alerted fighters. The 22 Wellingtons—two had left the inbound formation when engine problems plagued one—were at 15,000 ft (4,570 m) in a cloudless sky and with perfect visibility when they were first intercepted by Messerschmitt Bf109 fighters just south of Heligoland. When the Bf109 and Bf110 fighters broke off, heavy flak harassed the bombers at Bremerhaven, Wilhelmshaven, and the Schillig Roads. The fighters intercepted again beyond Wilhelmshaven, firing cannon at long range (600-900 yards/550-820 m), far beyond the defensive perimeter of the Wimpies' .303-cal (7.7 mm) machine guns.

One after another, the Wellingtons went down. Of 22 bombers engaged, ten made it back to England. The 12 doomed bombers with their 60 men represented a jolting loss of ten times the acceptable casualty rate.

That decisive raid was the third of three on the German Navy's lair. The first—on December 3—had been a great success; 24 Wellingtons fought their way through to bomb Heligoland, and all had returned. With heightened expectations, a force of a dozen Wellingtons repeated the foray December 14 but couldn't repeat the first success. The attackers lost five bombers to aggressive German fighter defenses and one more Wellington that crashed after it had crossed the Channel on the return trip.

The December 18 experience was the last straw. The official history of the RAF states: "From 18th December onwards we tacitly abandoned the belief that our Wellingtons and Hampdens could operate by day in the face of German fighter opposition." The bloody battles of December 14 and 18 over the Wilhelmshaven area had made a lie of the accepted truth that the bomber would always get through.

On the other side of the world, and more than two years later, the American experience was quite different. Air and naval forces had planned a daring combined operation to bomb the Japanese mainland. The strike force: 16 North American B-25B medium bombers, each carrying two 500 lb (227 kg) demolition bombs and 1,000 lb (454 kg) of incendiaries. The targets were military and industrial locations in the Tokyo—Yokohama, Osaka—Kobe, and Nagoya areas. The bombers were under the command of Lt. Col. James H. Doolittle, and he would lead the strike in the first airplane. The B-25s were to be based on the aircraft carrier USS *Hornet* and taken to within about 500 nautical miles (930 km) of the main islands of Japan. There they would fly from the carrier to their selected targets.

But a Japanese picketboat spotted the task force at 6:30 a.m. Tokyo time, much earlier than had been anticipated,

The North American B-25B Mitchell took off from the USS *Hornet* (CV-8) on April 18, 1942. (National Archives)

and the bombers had to take off earlier than intended. At 7:25 a.m. Tokyo time, on Saturday, April 18, 1942 (anniversary of the American Revolution's first battle at Lexington, Massachusetts, in 1776), the bombers roared from the pitching deck of the *Hornet*.

Japanese Army and Navy staffs believed the picket-boat reports but, having estimated the combat radius of American carrier-based aircraft at about 500 km (270 nautical miles), judged that an air strike could not come until the following day. The cautious defense commander, Army General Toshihiko-O Higashikuninomiya, ordered an alert for the Tokyo area at 8:30 a.m. Airborne training aircraft were ordered to land, and Ki27 and Ki15 aircraft, fully armed, were ordered into the air at about 10:00 a.m.

Navy commander of the Combined Fleet ordered readiness for attack against the U.S. task force at 7:50 a.m. Four G4M (Betty) attack bombers from Kisarazu *Kokutai* (Air Group) were sent out on scout duty. At 9:30 a.m., one of the G4M crew reported a B-25, identifying it as a flying boat of unknown nationality heading west, and "...faster than us." The Yokosuka *Kokutai* scrambled three Zeros to cover the Yokosuka naval port area.

As noon approached, the Ki27s began to land to refuel. Just after high noon, an observer post at Sugaya, north of Mito, reported that a large enemy plane had invaded Japanese airspace. And almost exactly at 12:15 p.m., the first B-25—Doolittle at the controls—dropped the first 500-pounder (227 kg bomb) on Tokyo.

Air-raid alarms went off in the city immediately, and about 40 Army fighters and reconnaissance aircraft scrambled to meet the attack. They climbed to altitude, because it was assumed that the bombers would be up there instead of on the deck. Among the Japanese defenders were four newly delivered Ki45-*Kai* (*Toryu*) twin-engined fighters. Japanese sources credit two Ki27s from the 5th *Hiko-Sentai* (Flying Regiment) and two from the 244th with making successful intercepts but without victory claims. An experimental Ki61 also intercepted and fired at a B-25.

Later crew reports from the American airmen told the story of the attack and of attempts made to thwart it.

Crew 3 (B-25B 40-2270, "Whiskey Pete"; target: Tokyo): intercepted by Japanese fighters after dropping the last bomb; top-turret gunner returned fire. B-25 was undamaged in the exchange and outran the fighters.

Crew 4 (B-25B 40-2282; target: Tokyo): at about 75 ft (23 m) altitude, was intercepted by two fixed-gear fighters (probably Nakajima Ki27). The bomber turned to fly under them, and its crew saw two more fighters at about 1,500 ft (460 m), ready to peel off and intercept. Bombs were salvoed, and the bomber turned to fly under the second pair. Another fighter tried an interception from the left front; that Japanese aircraft had an in-line engine and retractable gear (this may have been the experimental Ki61). This B-25 also outran the interceptors.

Crew 8 (B-25B 40-2242; target: Tokyo): a possible interception attempt, just before the target area, by a single fighter coming in on the bomber's right. Pilot unable to maneuver for a shot and was left behind.

Crew 9 (B-25B 40-2303, "The Whirling Dervish"; target: Tokyo): during bomb runs, a single fighter attacked from behind and below; engaged by the top-turret gunner and driven off, possibly hit.

Crew 10 (B-25B 40-2250; target: Tokyo): intercepted about 1.5 hr after takeoff at 500 ft (150 m) cruising altitude by a twin-engined patrol plane (probably Kawasaki Ki45-*Kai*) that dove to the attack. The B-25 pilot slammed on full power, dove underneath, and outran the Japanese plane. After bomb release, nine Zeros attacked from one o'clock high; again the pilot was able to dive and outrun them, redlining the B-25 at 330 mph (530 km/h) as he did so. Near Tokyo Bay on the outbound leg, three Ki27 fighters intercepted from 10 o'clock level, tried to catch the bomber, and failed. The Zeros hung on,

making occasional firing passes with no results, but broke off intercepts when the B-25 headed west for the mountains. A single fighter then intercepted and was driven off by gunfire from the B-25 turret and nose. Soon after, three Japanese fighters intercepted; the B-25 pilot used full power to climb into the cloud base and lost them. There were no further interceptions.

Crew 11 (B-25B 40-2249, "Hari Carrier"; target: Yokohama): about 30 miles (55 km) out from the target, and at about 500 ft (150 m) altitude, the B-25 was bounced by one fighter from a formation of four. The lone Japanese made two firing passes but was driven off by the B-25 turret gunner. As the bomber neared its target, a number of airplanes tried to intercept, but the B-25 evaded them. One last attempt was made by a single fighter during the bomb drop; the top-turret gunner fired and the fighter pulled up steeply, smoking heavily.

Crew 15 (B-25B 40-2267; target: Osaka—Kobe): after an intercept-free run-in and bomb drop, the B-25 was intercepted by a chance encounter with a pair of Ki27s more than an hour into the outbound trip toward China. The two gave chase but were easily outrun.

Most crew also reported heavy flak, but in general, all seem to have benefitted from the complete surprise of the attack and the speed of the B-25 compared to that of the obsolescent Ki27s that made up the predominant strength of the Japanese home defense air units.

But benefits attained on a single raid in 1942 could not be extrapolated to later bomber raids. The Doolittle effort, from start to finish, was in no way prototypical of later heavy bomber strikes against either the Japanese or the Germans. It did teach that low altitude, high-speed runs were one way of enhancing the safety of bomber operations, and that the element of surprise was still an effective adjunct.

Although the bombers got through this time, that luck would seldom be repeated in the hard years of war yet to come.

Nakajima Type 97 Model B fighters (Ki27B) of the 3rd *Chutai*, 5th *Hiko-Sentai*. The *Hiko-Sentai* was divided into three *Chutais*, and each *Chutai* was composed of 12 aircraft. (Yoji Watanabe)

British and German Air Defense Systems

The Royal Air Force had learned at high cost that daylight bombing by an unescorted formation of self-defending bombers was not the optimum way to hammer German military and industrial targets. That tactic would never again be a basic attack concept for Bomber Command.

Instead, the Command began its evolution of night-bombing tactics, developing them over the years of war into a well-honed and deadly weapon. To counter the ever-increasing effectiveness of British night raiders, Germany spent much of its effort and lost many pilots. In their turn, the Germans also developed night-bombing tactics. And the British had to spend effort and airmen to find a counter to the deadly harassment of nightly raids by forces of fast-moving medium bombers.

The *Luftwaffe* never did have a heavy bomber worthy of the name. Advocacy of that weapon had been spearheaded by *Luftwaffe Oberst* Walther Wever, who was killed in an airplane accident June 3, 1936. The concept effectively died with him. At the beginning of the expected brief war, the Germans saw no need for long-range strategic bombers. By the time events had made it clear that there was a demand for such a force, it was too late.

The early years of conflict between interceptors and heavy bombers were marked by the development, by both sides, of ground-based radars for early detection and interceptor control. Anti-aircraft artillery and "night" fighters—actually day fighters with experienced pilots—were the primary weapons. Searchlights sometimes helped, sometimes hindered, flak and fighters. Barrage balloons and observers were other components.

Then came airborne radar systems—and that's where this chapter will end. It begins with the state of the defenses in Germany and Great Britain when the bombing began.

In 1935 the *Luftwaffe* took over anti-aircraft artillery (*Fliegerabwehrkanonen=Flak*) used for defense of German airspace and built that branch of the service into an elite unit. When war came, *Flak* units were equipped with 3,000 searchlights and 9,300 guns, of which more than one-quarter were the versatile 8.8 cm cannon that could reach up to altitudes between 10,000 and 30,000 ft (3,000 and 9,000 m). Many of the guns and searchlights were deployed around Germany's major cities and the industrial targets of the Ruhr valley.

German defense commanders believed that searchlights would find and illuminate the bombers; anti-aircraft artillery would shoot them down. The layout of the defense zone would expose enemy aircraft to continuous fire for several minutes. It was good, in principle, but in practice, left something to be desired. Against a slow target at altitudes below 15,000 ft (4,570 m), the combination could score. Raise the speed and altitude of the attackers, and it was a new game. Besides, searchlights could only point wherever their crew steered them. Their effectiveness might be increased several folds if they knew where to look.

A way to look was being developed. Scientists had conceived the idea of using reflected radio waves to indicate the presence of a distant target. It might be a battleship—the original intent in some early experiments—or it might be an airplane.

Messerschmitt Bf109D of IV(N)/JG 2 (or 10(N)/JG 2) taxying at Jever airfield in the winter of 1939–40. (Bundesarchiv)

And so radar—Radio Detection and Ranging—became an asset to the defenses of the Third Reich. When the war began, eight *Freya* installations had been located along the North Sea coast; they were used only for early warning. But at that, the *Freya* sets were better, as was the system itself, than what the British had in place. Incredibly, there was no command and control center tied to the *Freya* chain, to receive and interpret its gathered data, and to dispatch interceptors. That function was left to informal contacts between searchers and interceptors until later.

There weren't many interceptors; the *Luftwaffe* had fielded only a single night-fighter unit—IV(N)/JG2[IV *Gruppe* (*Nacht*) of *Jagdgeschwader* 2], equipped with less than 50 Messerschmitt Bf109C and D aircraft—to work with searchlights and *Flak*. Within a month after the RAF night bombing attacks began in May 1940, it was obvious that German defenses were ineffective. Even Hermann Göring admitted that lack of night fighters was the Achilles' heel of the *Luftwaffe*.

The Bf109s returned to daylight operations, for which they were better suited, and the *Luftwaffe* began organizing and equipping a night fighter force with twin-engined, two-seat Bf110s. At night, those interceptors would have a better chance of detecting and destroying enemy bombers. They were able to carry heavier weapons, and they had four eyes in the cockpits instead of only two.

Meanwhile, a different kind of interception tactic had been developed and was about to be tested in combat. A handful of modified Dornier Do17Z-10 and Junkers Ju88C-2 aircraft was assigned to I/NJG2 (I *Gruppe* of *Nachtjagdgeschwader* 2), based at Gilze-Rijen in the Netherlands. Their mission: attack RAF bombers before they left base, or shoot them down in the landing pattern after a bombing raid. It was a successful tactic, and a frightening one to Bomber Command crew, whose nerves were tattered anyway after an evening over the Continent. The last thing they needed was trouble in the landing pattern. What saved them, as it saved Britain at the end of the Battle, was the German invasion of Russia. That operation drained every air and ground unit believed superfluous, and NJG2 was one such organization.

In October 1940, *Generalmajor* Josef Kammhuber was named General of Night Fighters. He poured additional searchlights, augmented by acoustic locators, into the German defenses, creating what has often been called the "Kammhuber Line." It covered the airspace from Belgium and the Netherlands down to the northern sectors of Germany, in a belt that varied between 50 and 100 miles (80 and 160 km) inland from

A GCI (Ground Control Interception) radar FuMG 62D *Würzburg* developed by Telefunken. (Bundesarchiv)

London

Lier

The Luftwaffe Defensive Night Fighting System
(December 31, 1941)

1. *Erg.* (Replacement *Staffel*) / NJG 2, Base: Gilze Rijen
2. II/NJG 2 except the 5th *Staffel*, Base: Leeuwarden
3. 5/NJG 2, Base: Wittmundhaven
4. 5/NJG 3, Base: Schleswig
5. 1/NJG 1, Base: St. Trond
6. I/NJG 1, except the 1st *Staffel*, Base: Venlo
7. *Stab* (Staff)/NJG 1, Base: Deelen
8. III/NJG 1, Base: Twente
9. I/NJG 3, except the 3rd *Staffel*, Base: Vechta
10. 7/NJG 3, Base: Lüneburg
11. I/NJG 1, Base: Bonn-Hangelar
12. II/NJG 3 except the 5th *Staffel*, Base: Mainz-Finthen
13. 3/NJG 3, Base: Werneuchen
14. *Erg.*/NJG 1, Base: Echterdingen
15. III/NJG 3 except the 8th *Staffel*, Base: Nellingen
16. 4/NJG 4, Base: Laupheim
17. 8/NJG 3, Base: Ingolstadt

Dark night fighting zone
(The "*Himmelbett*" zone)

Illuminated night fighting zone
(The "*Kammhuber* Line")

Combined night fighting zone

Operational
night fighter unit

Training
night fighter unit

RAF Heavy Bombers

Amsterdam

Command post of
XII *Fliegerkorps*
(command all night
fighter units)   Zeist   7

Bruxelles

Kiel

Hamburg

Bremen

Hannover

Dortmund

Düsseldorf

Köln (Cologne)

Berlin

Leipzig

Kassel

Dresden

Wiesbaden

Mannheim

Nürnberg

Strasbourg

München (Munich)

1

2

3

4

5

6

8

9

10

11

12

13

14

15

16

17

Messerschmitt Bf109G-6/R6 Cutaway

1 Engine-mounted 30 mm MK 108 cannon muzzle
2 Blast tube
3 Spinner
4 VDM9-12159 electrically-operated constant speed propeller
5 Propeller hub
6 Propeller pitch-change mechamism
7 Oil filler cap
8 Auxiliary cooling intakes
9 Oil tank (50 ltr/13.2 U.S. gal/11 gal)
10 Daimler Benz DB605AM 12-cylinder inverted-vee liquid cooled engine
11 Bleeder
12 Anti-vibration rubber engine mounting pads
13 Coolant filler cap
14 Coolant header tank
15 Plug leads

16 Exhaust stubs
17 Oil cooler
18 Rheinmetall Borsig 13 mm MG 131 machine guns
19 Ignition magnet
20 Electron forged engine bearer
21 Filter covered inpeller
22 Supercharger air intake
23 Machine gun mount
24 MG 131 ammunition feed chute
25 Engine control rods
26 MK 108 ammunition belt
27 Rheinmetall Borsig 30 mm MK 108 cannon
28 Port rudder pedal
29 90 mm armorglass windscreen
30 Revi 16B reflector gunsight
31 Instrument panel
32 Cockpit ventilation inlet
33 Canopy
34 Flamed armorglass head/back panel
35 Seat harness
36 8 mm back-armored pilot's seat
37 Horizontal stabilizer trim handwheel (inboard)
38 Undercarriage retraction cables
39 Undercarriage emergency retraction handwheel (outboard)
40 Horizontal stabilizer trimming cables

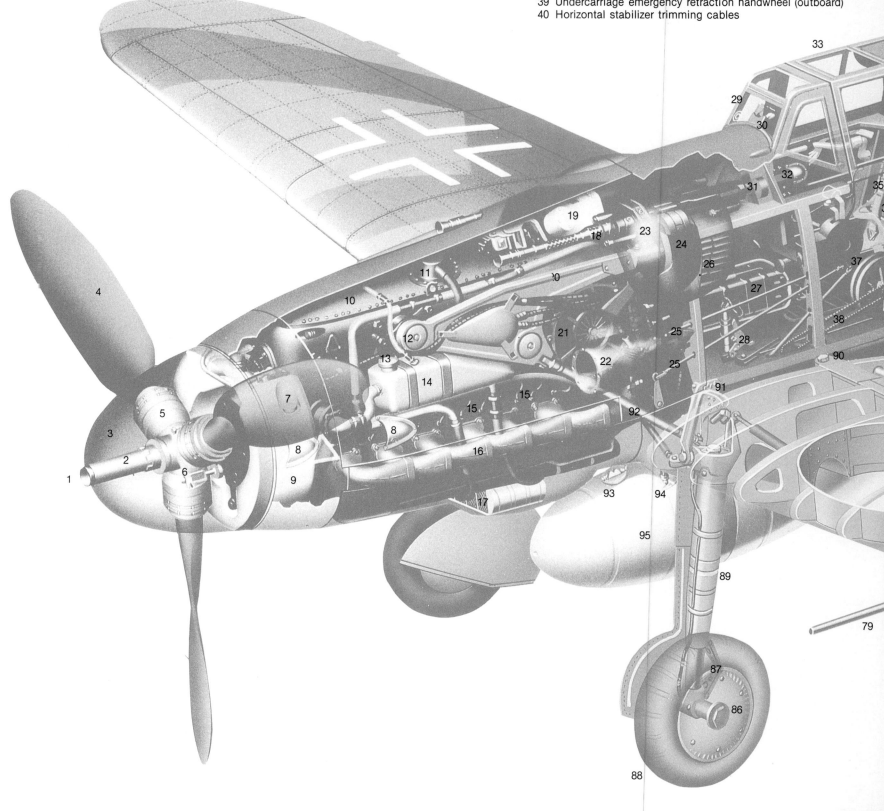

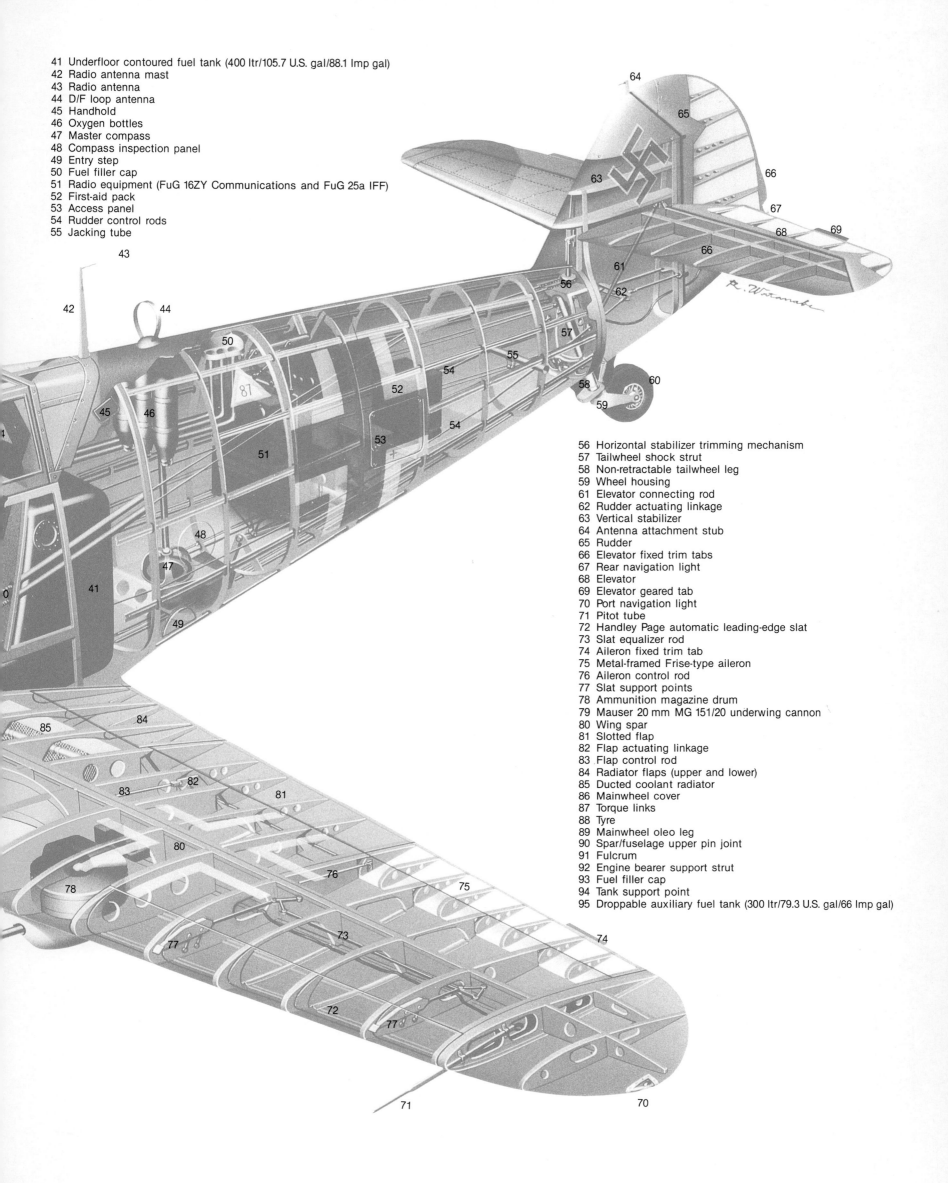

41 Underfloor contoured fuel tank (400 ltr/105.7 U.S. gal/88.1 Imp gal)
42 Radio antenna mast
43 Radio antenna
44 D/F loop antenna
45 Handhold
46 Oxygen bottles
47 Master compass
48 Compass inspection panel
49 Entry step
50 Fuel filler cap
51 Radio equipment (FuG 16ZY Communications and FuG 25a IFF)
52 First-aid pack
53 Access panel
54 Rudder control rods
55 Jacking tube

56 Horizontal stabilizer trimming mechanism
57 Tailwheel shock strut
58 Non-retractable tailwheel leg
59 Wheel housing
61 Elevator connecting rod
62 Rudder actuating linkage
63 Vertical stabilizer
64 Antenna attachment stub
65 Rudder
66 Elevator fixed trim tabs
67 Rear navigation light
68 Elevator
69 Elevator geared tab
70 Port navigation light
71 Pitot tube
72 Handley Page automatic leading-edge slat
73 Slat equalizer rod
74 Aileron fixed trim tab
75 Metal-framed Frise-type aileron
76 Aileron control rod
77 Slat support points
78 Ammunition magazine drum
79 Mauser 20 mm MG 151/20 underwing cannon
80 Wing spar
81 Slotted flap
82 Flap actuating linkage
83 Flap control rod
84 Radiator flaps (upper and lower)
85 Ducted coolant radiator
86 Mainwheel cover
87 Torque links
88 Tyre
89 Mainwheel oleo leg
90 Spar/fuselage upper pin joint
91 Fulcrum
92 Engine bearer support strut
93 Fuel filler cap
94 Tank support point
95 Droppable auxiliary fuel tank (300 ltr/79.3 U.S. gal/66 Imp gal)

The Junkers Ju88C-4 of I/NJG 2 made a forced landing after a night intruder sortie against RAF bomber base in 1941. (Bundesarchiv)

the North Sea and the English Channel coasts. Working as an integral part of that defense system were the night fighters, flying airborne patrols and waiting to be directed toward bombers that had been found by the searchlights, and that were likely to be silhouetted against fire, flares, or the searchlights' glare.

It was a temporary defense, at best, and Kammhuber's next step was much more permanent and potentially far deadlier to the bombers. The night fighters, which formerly had been called in to intercept over a target area, were redirected to intercept in areas clear of the cities and industrial targets, protecting German airmen from the hazards of concentrated friendly fire. Ground-control radars were stationed every 36 km (22 mls) to straddle the inbound routes used by British bombers headed for the Ruhr and beyond. Each radar site had three basic units: one *Freya*, for early detection and surveillance, and two *Würzburg* tracking units, one to follow an incoming bomber and the other to track its attacking interceptor. Tracks from both were plotted, and controllers directed fighters toward targets.

The British countered by streaming bombers through the line in droves, saturating the defenses. Kammhuber's next move increased the number of radar sites, introduced improved tracking radar (*Würzburg Riese*), and pushed development of air interception radars for night fighters.

For a while, the Germans had the upper hand; then, on a raid to Hamburg on July 24, 1943, RAF bomber crews tossed out packets of "window," radar-reflecting strips of aluminum that created bright and blossoming returns, masking

the bomber's blips on the screens of German radars. It was a most effective countermeasure, and it drove the Germans to a complete rethinking and revision of their night intercept tactics.

Luftwaffe Major Hajo Herrmann proposed the idea of concentrating interceptors above the target, rather than having ground controllers direct them to intercepts. He also suggested that flak shells be fused to burst below the altitudes at which the interceptors patrolled. Because the radar was effectively nullified by "window," the interceptors would make visual contacts and intercepts, then dive into the bomber stream to attack. At that point, they would be vulnerable to friendly fire. But the risk was deemed worthwhile and, perhaps seeing a parallel to the bravery of the beast, the experiment took the code name of *Wilde Sau* (Wild Boar).

Hermann organized an experimental unit, which later became *Jagdgeschwader* 300, in late June 1943. Equipped with Bf109G-6 and Fw190A-5 interceptors, JG300 operated from Bonn-Hangelar. Soon after, JG301 and JG302 formed, operating from Neubiberg, near München, and Döberitz, near Berlin. The units were under-equipped; only one *Gruppe*—about 36 aircraft—in each *Geschwader* had its own interceptor aircraft; the other two *Gruppen* shared the Bf109G-6 day fighters based at the same airfields.

Wilde Sau lasted only a few months; aircraft attrition was high, in part due to the extreme utilization rate of the fighters, rotated among pilots from three *Staffeln*. By late 1943, its days were numbered, and its pilots began retraining as day fighters.

By this time, German airborne radar and radio direction-finding equipment was available in quantities sufficient for widespread operational use, and the first *Staffeln* so equipped were operational. That development is the subject of a later chapter.

The British Radio Direction Finding group had an operational prototype radar station operating by mid-1935 and, by the end of that year, was routinely detecting aircraft the size of fighters at ranges of 50 miles (80 km). That accomplishment convinced officials that radar was the keystone of an air defense system, and planning began for a chain of stations covering the likely overwater approaches from Germany.

When war started in September 1939, the Chain

A black-finished Bf110E-1 flown by *Oberleutnant* Hans-Karl Kamp (23 victories), *Staffelkapitän* of 7/NJG 4, flying over Western Europe. (Bundesarchiv)

Home early detection radar system was in operation with 17 units sited along the English coast between Land's End and Newcastle. Other stations were added later to cover the western and northern approaches. Further, the concept of a group operations room—actually a command and control center—had been developed and existed in prototype. It included a filter room, where trained operators first screened the raw radar data, and interpreted it as indications of enemy or friendly forces.

Detection systems and techniques had improved, and detection ranges now stretched out to 100 miles (160 km). Once received, the reflected signals from an incoming bomber attack were interpreted in the filter room, assigned a designation, and indicated by visual plots on a large mapping table. The information was passed to Group and Sector operations units, as well as to Fighter Command.

The Chain Home system worked until bombers crossed the coast and headed inland; then, of course, they were lost to radar sights fixed seaward. Supplementary sightings came from another vital component of the air defense system: the Observer Corps, a volunteer group of airplane spotters whose services and knowledge were invaluable, and whose contribution was recognized in 1941 by the award of the "Royal" designation. Operationally, observers tracked incoming raids visually and reported them to the Group operations room by telephone, while also keeping track of the plots in an Observer center.

Another key element in Britain's defenses was a relatively simple radio direction-finding technique called "Pip-Squeak," an airborne device that automatically switched on a fighter aircraft's high-frequency radio transmitter continuously for 14 seconds in every minute. Ground-based direction-finding (DF) stations received the signal, took bearings, and by triangulation, plotted the fighter's position very accurately. By sequencing the time of the transmissions, four fighters could be tracked by a single DF station. Radar and Pip-Squeak were, it has been stated, the key to all interceptions made by Fighter Command.

Anti-aircraft artillery, searchlights, and barrage balloon barriers also were part of the British air defenses. Balloons and searchlights channeled the attackers, anti-aircraft artillery harassed them at worst, destroyed them at best, and fighters intercepted those that got through. AA guns were sited to protect cities and industrial targets; many were concentrated in a belt southeast of London, near the coast, chosen to get the earliest possible shots at incoming attacks. Statistics available for AA strength, before the Battle of Britain began in August 1940, show 1,177 heavy guns, 574 light guns, and 3,033 light machine guns. The latter were effectively useless except for harassment fire from point target systems like searchlight units.

The interceptors—the basic weapon of Britain's air defense system—were the Hawker Hurricane and the Supermarine Spitfire, two fighters designed to a 1934 specification for eight-gun platforms. (The eight .303-caliber/7.7 mm machine guns were not British; they were American Colt designs, built under license in Britain.) In June 1940, Fighter Command mustered about 575 fighters, predominantly Hurricanes and Spitfires, but including a few Gloster Gladiator biplanes. There were nearly 1,100 pilots rated on these types then, or about two pilots for each aircraft.

German bomber fleets, numbering about 1,000 long-range bombers and 250 dive-bombers, had begun attacks

No. 85 Squadron's Hawker Hurricane Mk I waits for the coming night's work against German raiders. (Imperial War Museum)

against the British Isles on the night of June 5, 1940. The debacle on the Continent was over; Dunkirk had been evacuated, Hitler still planned to invade Britain. Göring promised quick submission of Britain, and ordered the bombers to attack.

The British defenses, complete though they may have seemed, had some severe drawbacks. Over land, said Winston Churchill, the defenses were "…Early Stone Age." The Chain Home radars produced very accurate bearing data, but were not reliable sources of either altitude or strength data. The British had no strong night fighter force, although a handful of Bristol Blenheim night fighters, equipped with airborne intercept radar, were operational. One scored the first victory for airborne radar when it destroyed a German bomber during the night of July 22.

The Germans dispatched unescorted bomber forces of 60 or 70 aircraft, at night, and lost only one or two to the sporadic and ineffective interceptions by day fighters working with difficulty against great handicaps. These kinds of attacks continued during June and July. Then in August, a band of good weather was forecast, and the *Luftwaffe* command ordered a major attack at 7:00 a.m., August 13. To blunt British defenses, the Germans planned an air assault for August 12, aimed at destroying all the known British radar stations. Then, having blinded the primary source of interception information, the Germans planned to bomb Fighter Command coastal airfields, destroying aircraft and making runways unserviceable.

On August 12 the attacks came, fighters intercepted and fought, bombs destroyed some radars, holed some runways. But when the smoke had cleared, and the damage totaled, the British defenses had been bloodied, but not beaten. Bombed radar stations were back on the air in 24 to 72 hours; runways were used again the next day. British fighter losses totaled 32; German bomber losses, 48.

The mid-August bombing strikes by the *Luftwaffe* failed in their objectives. The British also were aided by a stupid command decision passed along—or originated—by Göring. Furious because of bomber losses during the previous days, he ordered the *Luftwaffe*'s escorting fighters to stay even closer to the bombers, to defend them from interception. But most of the British fighters destroyed during the previous intensive air fighting had fallen to the guns of Bf109s in free-chase by fighters free to attack. By demanding that the bombers' fighter escort stay in defensive positions, Göring ensured that RAF Fighter Command would gain valuable experience in defeating bomber swarms.

There's an interesting footnote: also on August 12, the first Bristol Beaufighter night fighter was delivered from the factory at Filton to the RAF Fighter Interception Unit at Tangmere. It was the first of a new generation of British night fighters, and it carried an advanced air interception (AI) radar.

Hun in the Sun

One hopes the derogatory term will be forgiven after the passing of years. It refers to an earlier time when Allied pilots flew toward the East on early morning patrols during World War I. German pilots had the morning sun at their backs, hence the caution to inexperienced Allied pilots: "Beware the Hun in the sun."

To the daylight bombers of a later war, the warning still was appropriate. A bomber formation, high over Germany and headed for a target, came under continuing attack by determined *Luftwaffe* pilots who could choose the time and the approach avenue. They too came out of the sun.

They came with a variety of weapons and with a number of versatile and ever-changing tactics. Their first experiences had been against daylight strikes by light bombers of Britain's Advance Air Striking Force, a mix of Bristol Blenheims and Fairey Battles, both unsuited for the tasks facing them, but flown nevertheless into the maelstrom of modern air war.

But the *Luftwaffe* got its fill of daytime fighting when the USAAF began its bombing strikes against targets in the German homeland. And that experience of *Luftwaffe* day interceptors against USAAF heavy bombers comprises the body of this chapter.

The basic document that guided U.S. airmen against Germany was Air War Plans Division Plan No. 42, modifying an earlier plan to match the realities of war. Beating Germany was the first priority; defeating Japan would come later. The first three objectives of AWPD-42 were "...(a) defeat the German air force; (b) destroy the sources of German submarine construction; (c) undermine the German war-making capacity." Submarine yards, transportation systems, electrical power systems, and oil plants were primary targets. Assembly plants for fighters, bombers, and aircraft engines, in that order, were intermediate targets with overriding priority.

Thousands of U.S. Boeing B-17 and Consolidated B-24 bombers were employed to those ends over a two-year period. Their tactics changed continually. Their daytime missions, combined with the nighttime missions of RAF Bomber Command, spurred development of a panoply of new German weapons and interception tactics, and eventually devastated, but did not defeat unaided, the Third Reich.

The USAAF's first heavy bomber foray against the continent was made August 17, 1942. The 97th Bomb Group dispatched a dozen B-17Es to bomb Rouen-Sotteville in occupied France and six to create a diversion. They dropped 600 lb (272 kg) and 1,100 lb (499 kg) general-purpose bombs. Gunners claimed to have hit one enemy aircraft; two bombers received minor damage.

Four days later, 12 B-17Es from the 97th BG headed for Rotterdam. They were late at the rendezvous; their fighter escort turned back home early. Then, about 25 *Luftwaffe* fighters attacked, damaging one bomber, killing one crewman, and wounding five others. The bombers also turned back, having been recalled as they crossed the French coast inbound.

Through the late summer, Eighth Air Force bombers gained in strength and experience and learned about *Luftwaffe* interception tactics the hard way. In the heat of battle, bomber gunners saw every smoking fighter as proof of its destruction, not realizing that German fuel was of poor quality and that engines smoked when *Luftwaffe* pilots suddenly rammed throttles open.

Exaggerated claims aside, USAAF bomber defenses were much stronger than those of RAF bombers, the *Luft-*

Focke-Wulf Fw190A-3s of 7/JG 2 scramble from airfield in France to intercept a daylight raid in 1942. (Bundesarchiv)

Consolidated B-24H-5 Liberator

of the 448th BG, 847BS, 8th AF, based at
Seething, England in February 1944.

Power units
  4 × Pratt & Whitney R-1830-65 Twin Wasp 14-cylinder
  air-cooled engines: 1,200 hp each at 26,500 ft (8,080 m)

Dimensions
  Span: 110 ft 0 in (33.53 m)
  Length, level position: 67 ft 2 in (20.47 m)
  Height, on the ground: 18 ft 0 in (5.49 m)
  Wing area: 1,048 sq ft (97.4 m²)
Weights
  Empty: 36,500 lb (16,560 kg)
  Gross: 56,000 lb (25,400 kg)
Performance
  Max speed: 300 mph (483 km/h) at 30,000 ft (9,140 m)
  Service ceiling: 30,000 ft (9,140 m)
  Range with 5,000 lb (2,270 kg) bombs: 2,100 mls (3,380 km)
Armament
  Defensive fire: 10 × 0.5 in (12.7 mm) Browning M2 machine guns
                   with 4,700 rounds in all
  Bombs: 12,800 lb (5,810 kg)
Crew 10

Focke-Wulf

of II/JG 1 bas
in early 1944.

Power unit
  Bayerische Motor
  engine: 1,700 hp f
  1,440 hp at 5,700 m
Dimensions
  Span: 10.506 n (34
  Length, tail up 8.95
  Height, tail down, o
  Wing area: 183 m² (1

Avro Lancaster B Mk I

of No. 57 Squadron based at East Kirby, Lincolnshire,
in February 1945.

Power units
  4 × Rolls-Royce Merlin XX or 22 12-cylinder liquid-cooled engines:
  1,460 hp each at 6,250 ft (1,905 m)
Dimensions
  Span: 102 ft 0 in (31.09 m)
  Length, tail up: 69 ft 6 in (21.18 m)
  Height, tail up: 20 ft 6 in (6.25 m)
  Wing area: 1,300 sq ft (120.8 m²)
Weights
  Empty: 41,000 lb (18,600 kg)
  Gross: 68,000 lb (30,840 kg)
Performance
  Max speed: 281 mph (452 km/h) at 11,000 ft (3,350 m)
  Service ceiling: 24,500 ft (7,470 m)
  Range with 10,000 lb (4,540 kg) bombs: 1,040 mls (1,670 km)
Armament
  Defensive fire: 8 × 0.303 in (7.7 mm) Browning machine guns with 14,000 rounds in all
  Bombs: 14,000 lb (6,350 kg)
Crew 7

Messerschmitt Bf110G-4/R3/R8/R22

flown by *Oberstleutnant* Hans-Joachim Jabs,
Kommodore of NJG 1, at Lüneburg, Germany
in April 1945. He scored 22 day and 28 night
victories during 710 missions.

Power units
  2 × Daimler-Benz DB605B-1 12-cylinder liquid-cooled
  engines: 1,475 hp each for take-off,
  1,355 hp each at 5,700 m (18,700 ft)
Dimensions
  Span: 16.25 m (53 ft 3¹³/₁₆ in)
  Length, without radar antennas: 12.07 m (39 ft 7³/₁₆ in)
  Height: 4.18 m (13 ft 8⁹/₁₆ in)
  Wing area: 38.4 m² (413.4 sq ft)

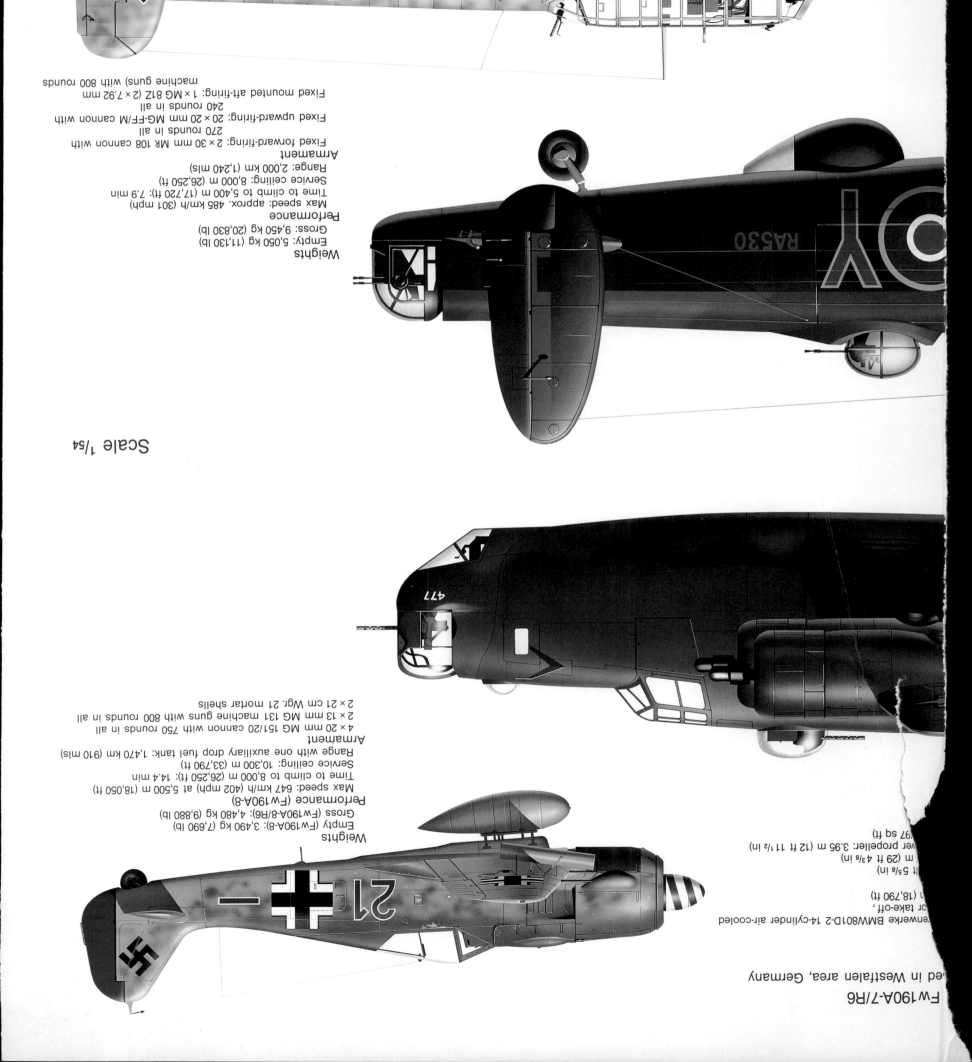

Electronic equipment
Airborne interception radar: FuG 218 *Neptun*
Crew 3

Fixed mounted aft-firing: 1 × MG 81Z (2 × 7.92 mm
machine guns) with 800 rounds

Fixed upward-firing: 20 × 20 mm MG-FF/M cannon with
240 rounds in all

Fixed forward-firing: 2 × 30 mm MK 108 cannon with
270 rounds in all

Armament

Range: 2,000 km (1,240 mls)
Service ceiling: 8,000 m (26,250 ft)
Time to climb to 5,400 m (17,720 ft): 7.9 min
Max speed: approx. 485 km/h (301 mph)

Performance

Gross: 9,450 kg (20,830 lb)
Empty: 5,050 kg (11,130 lb)

Weights

Scale 1/54

2 × 21 cm Wgr. 21 mortar shells
2 × 13 mm MG 131 machine guns with 800 rounds in all
4 × 20 mm MG 151/20 cannon with 750 rounds in all

Armament

Range with one auxiliary drop fuel tank: 1,470 km (910 mls)
Service ceiling: 10,300 m (33,790 ft)
Time to climb to 8,000 m (26,250 ft): 14.4 min
Max speed: 647 km/h (402 mph) at 5,500 m (18,050 ft)

Performance (Fw190A-8)

Gross (Fw190A-8/R6): 4,480 kg (9,880 lb)
Empty (Fw190A-8): 3,490 kg (7,690 lb)

Weights

97 sq ft)
ver propeller: 3.95 m (12 ft 11½ in)
m (29 ft 4³/₈ in)
ft 5⁵/₈ in)
n (18,790 ft)
or take-off,
enwerke BMW801D-2 14-cylinder air-cooled

ed in Westfalen area, Germany

Fw190A-7/R6

Ju88C-2 of 2/NJG 2 at Catania, Sicilia in December, 1941.

Ju88 C-6 of 1/NJG 100 on the Eastern Front in 1943.

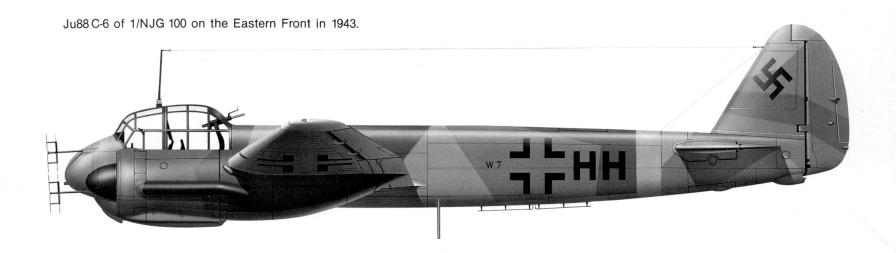

Ju88R-2 of 8/NJG2 in the western part of Germany, autumn of 1944.

Ju88 G-1 of 3/NJG 7 flown by *Oberfeldwebel* Jakob Schultz at Vaerlöse in Denmark. Made a forced landing at Bultofta in Sweden on October 6, 1944 (shortly before redesignated to IV/NJG 2).

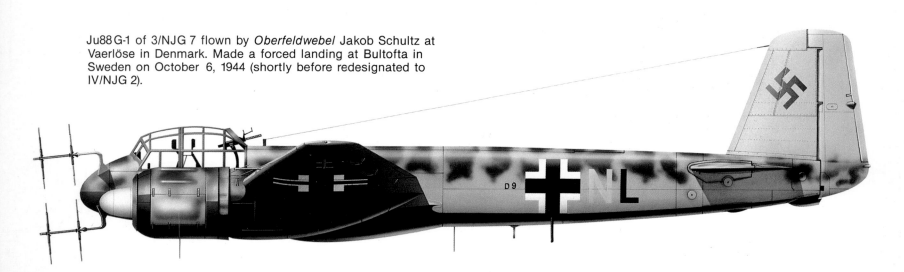

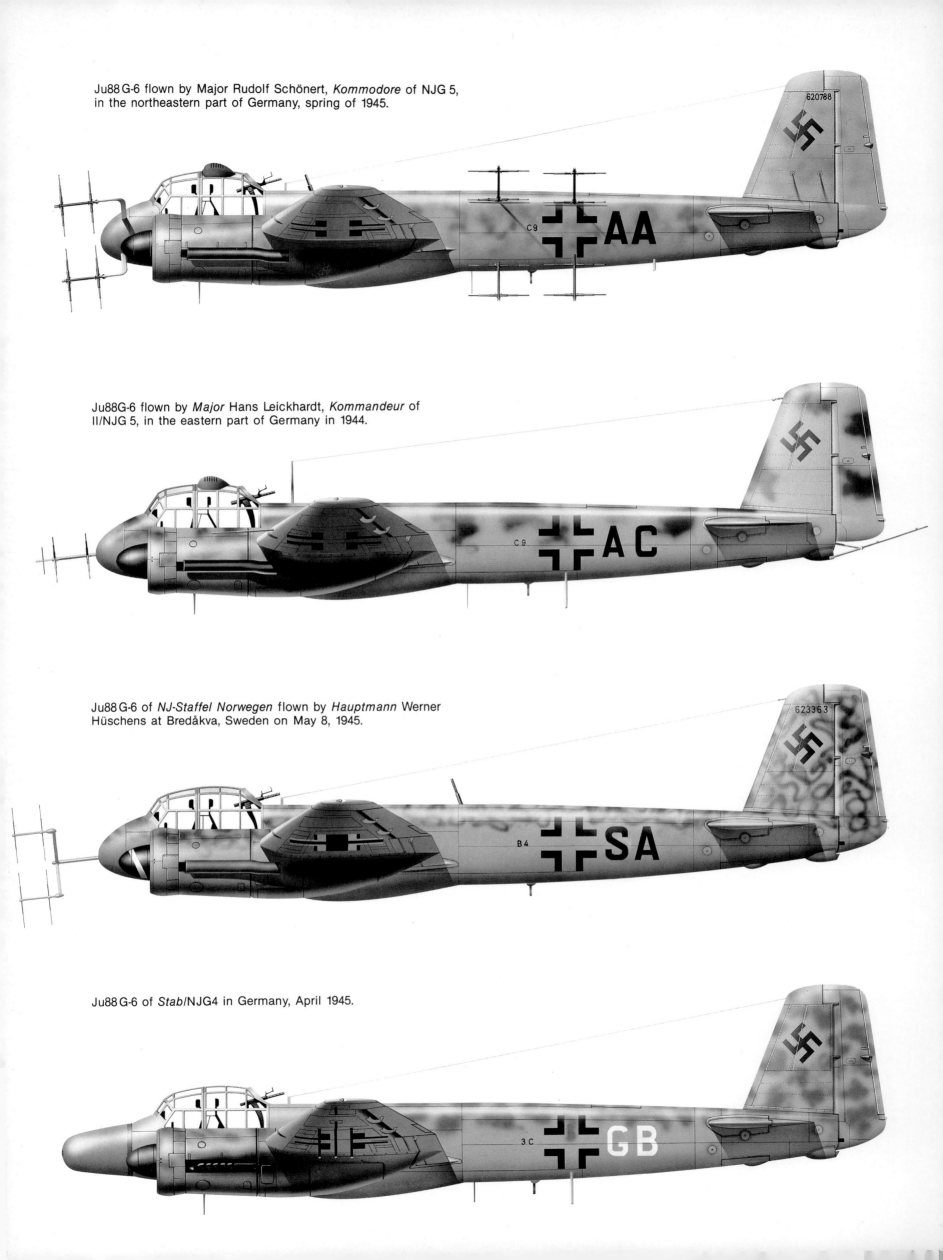

Ju88 G-6 flown by Major Rudolf Schönert, *Kommodore* of NJG 5, in the northeastern part of Germany, spring of 1945.

Ju88 G-6 flown by *Major* Hans Leickhardt, *Kommandeur* of II/NJG 5, in the eastern part of Germany in 1944.

Ju88 G-6 of *NJ-Staffel Norwegen* flown by *Hauptmann* Werner Hüschens at Bredåkva, Sweden on May 8, 1945.

Ju88 G-6 of *Stab*/NJG4 in Germany, April 1945.

Ju88C-2

Power units
: 2 × 1,175 hp (for take-off) Jumo 211/B-1 liquid-cooled engines

Dimensions
Span: 18.25 m (59 ft 10½ in)
Length, tail up: 14.35 m (47 ft 1 in)
Height, tail up: 5.30 m (17 ft 4¹¹/₁₆ in)
Wing area: 52.5 m² (565.1 sq ft)

Weights
Max take-off: 11,000 kg (24,250 lb)

Performance
Max speed: 475 km/h (295 mph) at 5,500 m (18,050 ft)
Range: 1,820 km (1,130 mls)

Armament
Fixed forward-firing: 1 × 20 mm MG-FF/M cannon, 3 × 7.92 mm MG 17 machine guns
Flexible mounted aft-firing: 2 × 7.92 mm MG 15 machine guns

Ju88C-6

Power units
: 2 × 1,420 hp (for take-off) Jumo 211J liquid-cooled engines

Dimensions
Span: 20.08 m (65 ft 10⁹/₁₆ in)
Length without radar aerials, tail up: 14.96 m (49 ft 1 in)
Height, tail up: 5.07 m (16 ft 7⁹/₁₆ in)
Wing area: 54.7 m² (588.8 sq ft)

Weights
Max take-off: 11,450 kg (25,240 lb)

Performance
Max speed: 500 km/h (311 mph) at 5,300 m (17,390 m)
Range: 2,950 km (4,750 mls)

Armament
Fixed forward-firing: 1 × 20 mm MG 151/20 or 20 mm MG-FF/M cannon
2 × 20 mm MG-FF/M cannon
3 × 7.92 mm MG 17 machine guns
Flexible mounted aft-firing: 1 × 13 mm MG 131 machine gun

Electronic equipment
Airborne interception radar:
FuG 202 Lichtenstein BC or FuG 212 Lichtenstein C-1

Ju88R-2

Power units
: 2 × 1,700 hp (for take-off) BMW 80/D-2 air-cooled engines

Dimensions
: same as Ju88C-6

Weight
Max take-off: 11,500 kg (25,350 lb)

Performance
Max speed: 500 km/h (311 mph) at 6,000 m (19,690 ft)
Range: 2,000 km (1,240 mls)

Armament
: same as Ju 88C-6

Electronic equipment
Airborne interception radar: FuG 220 Lichtenstein SN-2

Ju88G-1

Power units
: 2 × 1,700 hp (for take-off) BMW 801D-2 air-cooled engines

Dimensions
Span, Height and wing area: same as Ju88C-6
Length without radar aerials, tail up: 15.50 m (50 ft 10¹/₄ in)

Weight
Max take-off: 12,100 kg (26,680 lb)

Performance
Max speed: 520 km/h 323 mph) at 6,000 m (19,690 ft)
Range: 2,800 km (1,740 mls)

Armament
Fixed forward-firing: 4 × 20 mm MG 151/20 cannon
Flexible mounted aft-firing: 1 × 13 mm MG 131 machine gun

Electronic equipments
Airborne interception radar: FuG 220 Lichtenstein SN-2
Passive homing device: FuG 227 Flensburg (aerials fitted under the wings)

Ju88G-6

Power units
: 2 × 1,750 hp (for take-off) Jumo 2⁻3A liquid-cooled engines

Dimensions
: same as Ju88G-1

Weight
Max take-off: 12,400 kg (27,340 lb)

Performance
Max speed: 540 km/h (336 mph) at 6,000 m (19,690 ft)
Range: 2,200 km (1,370 mls)

Armament
Fixed forward-firing: 4 × 20 mm MG 151/20 cannon
Fixed upward-firing: 2 × 20 mm MG 151/20 cannon
Flexible mounted aft-firing: 1 × 13 mm MG 131 machine gun

Electronic equipments
Airborne interception radar: FuG 220 Lichtenstein SN-2 with special vertical installation
Passive homing/warning device: FuG 350 Naxos ZR (aerial fitted on the canopy)

Ju88G-6

Armament: same as Ju88G-1

Electronic equipments
Airborne interception/tail-warning radar: FuG 228 Lichtenstein SN-3
Passive homing/warning device: FuG 350 Naxos Z

Ju88G-6

Armament: same as Ju88G-6

Electronic equipments
Airborne interception radar: FuG 213 Neptun

Ju88G-6

Armament: same as Ju88G-1

Electronic equipments
Airborne interception radar: FuG 240/1 Berlin N-1a
Radio altimeter: FuG 101 (aerials fitted under the wings)

---

waffe's earlier targets. German airmen recognized the cumulative strength of a tightly held bomber formation. So, they reasoned, breaking up the formation would be a tactical advantage. That done, they could deal with individual bombers more successfully.

The development of tactics to break bomber formations included, as an early attempt, air-to-air bombing. The first such attack recorded was made by a pair of Focke-Wulf Fw190s on February 16, 1943, during a mission against submarine yards at St. Nazaire. The fighters dove from above and behind a B-17 formation and, when they were about 150 feet (50 m) above the bombers, dropped clusters of time-fused fragmentation bombs. The bombs detonated behind the bombers, although at the same level, doing minimum damage.

But such tactics were of small value compared to the basic intercepts and attacks by aggressive Luftwaffe pilots in standard Bf109s and Fw190s. They went to school on successive formations of B-17s; every sortie taught something new. Gaining in experience, the fighters pressed home the assault and began to hurt the bombers. The mission of April 17 to Bremen saw 107 B-17s from four Bomb Groups hammered by well-organized and well-coordinated Fw190s. Wave after wave of the snub-nosed fighters bored in, and when the shooting stopped, 16 bombers were down, a loss rate of nearly 15 percent. It was far worse than for any earlier mission and signalled to the USAAF for the first time that perhaps bombers alone were not as effective a fighting defense force as had been thought.

By then, bomber missions were being escorted by Republic P-47 Thunderbolt fighters. But their range was limited by internal fuel capacity, and as a result, the escort had to turn back before the bombers reached the target. The plan was that another escort force would meet the bombers at about the same place on their return. But the reality was that bombers still went alone to the target and its fierce defenses.

An abortive attempt was made to provide modified B-17 bombers as escorts. Designated YB-40s, these aircraft carried no bombs. Instead, the standard top, belly, and tail turret installations were augmented by an extra top turret, a new two-gun chin turret, 14 power-driven .50-cal (12.7 mm) machine guns, and 11,000 rounds of ammunition. All that weight worked against performance, and the YB-40s were unable to keep up with combat formations traveling light after bomb drops.

The Germans added a new airborne weapon in July, the Werfergranaten Wgr. 21, a large-caliber, rocket-propelled mortar shell. It was an adaptation of a standard infantry mortar shell, 21 cm (a little larger than 8 in) in diameter, weighed 80 kg (176 lb), and was launched from a simple tube mounted under the outboard wing section of German fighters (usually Bf109, Bf110, and Fw190 types). Its flight speed was about 320 m (1,050 ft) /sec, and it was usually fired from distances of 1,200 or 1,400 m (1,310 or 1,530 yards), well outside the range of bomber defenses. It was not a precision weapon; it was intended to scatter the bombers and break their massed defenses. Its first reported use was against the 385th BG during a mission over Oschersleben. The unguided missile hit a B-17, which blew apart, its fragments taking two other bombers down with it.

By autumn, modified Fw190A-4/R6 fighters, with armament that included the Wgr. 21, were systematically used

Air battle over Bremen on November 13, 1943. A Fw190A (extreme right, top) attacks on Boeing B-17F Flying Fortresses of the 8th Air Force. The 8th AF lost 16 heavy bombers in this mission. (USAF)

as the first wave in fighter attacks. Waves of standard Fw190s and Bf109s followed through. These tactics, along with others, were used during the long-range mission against Schweinfurt on October 14, 1943. It was the second raid on that city, and the *Luftwaffe* hit the unescorted bomber formations hard. Out of 291 bombers dispatched, 227 attacked the targets. The losses were staggering; 60 bombers down, with their 600 men, and 142 other bombers damaged severely, many never to fly again. That loss rate of 26 percent ended unescorted day bombing by the USAAF. The bombers did not always get through.

In the aftermath of that aerial disaster, Third Bombardment Division of the VIII Bomber Command, USAAF, analyzed more than 2,500 separate attacks against its bombers during the previous six months, classified them by types, and published the results in Special Informational Intelligence Report No. 43-17.

The attack tactics were called by descriptive names: The Rocketeers, The Triple Threat, Tail Gunner's Headache, The Roller Coaster, The Pepper Spray, The Sister Act, The Swooper, The Twin-Engine Tail-Pecker. They were all variations on a basic theme that *Luftwaffe* pilots had been playing since the first attacks.

Those first attacks were made in the time-honored manner: approach from six o'clock, and shoot. It had worked before, but it didn't work in the face of heavy machine guns in tail turrets. Plan B: attack the other end of the formation, where the defenses were weaker. Fighters intercepted bomber groups and flew alongside or behind, out of range, gauging speed and altitude as gunnery guides. Then they overtook and passed the formation and, when well out in front, turned to attack. It sounds easy; but the closing speed between 175 mph (280 km/h) bombers and 300 mph (480 km/h) fighters is 475 mph (760 km/h), leaving a very brief time to aim, fire, and break away. If, for example, a *Luftwaffe* pilot opened fire at 500 yards (450 m) and broke away at 100 (90 m), he had less than two seconds to complete one attack. (Count mentally, now: One thousand one, one thousand two. That's two seconds; would you do everything right?)

Chronologically, the next attack concept was the rocket barrage of 21 cm mortar shells. Fighters so armed lobbed their rounds in from the rear or abeam, hoping to disrupt the steady flight of the bomber formations.

Escort fighters were, of course, the answer. What made them practical was the drop tank, a simple but invaluable

A Messerschmitt Bf109G-6 fitted with Wgr. 21 rocket tubes. (Bundesarchiv)

A close-up of a rocket tube installed under the wing of Bf109G-6/Trop. (Bundesarchiv)

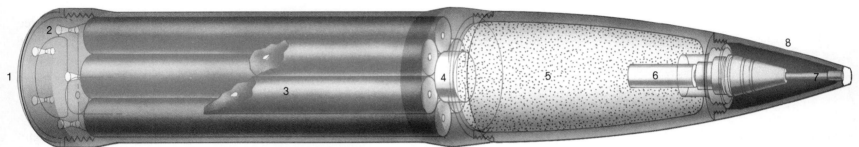

Wgr. 21 (21 cm *Wurfgranate* 42 *Sprengladung*)
air-to-air rocket-propelled mortar shell

Diameter: 214 mm (8 7/16 in)
Length overall: 1,260 mm (4 ft 1 5/8 in)
Total weight: 110 kg (243 lb)
Weight of explosive filling: 9.5 kg (20.9 lb)
Muzzle velocity: 320 m (1,050 ft)/sec
Range: 500-7,850 m (550-8,585 yds)
Most effective range: 1,200–1,400 m (1,310–1,530 yds)

1 Closing plate
2 Venturi
3 Propellant charge
4 Head igniter
5 High explosive filling
6 Booster
7 Fuze
8 Windshield

scheme for increasing the range of short-ranged fighters. P-47s and Lockheed P-38 Lightnings used them and were able to escort bombers all the way to some of their targets. The Thunderbolts first went all the way with the bombers against Emden on September 27, 1943, a few days before the second Schweinfurt fiasco. The P-38s first went to Wilhelmshaven as an escort force on November 3.

But it was the brilliantly conceived and designed North American P-51 Mustang that really turned the tide. Its advanced aerodynamics, coupled with drop tanks, gave it the range to go anywhere in Germany, even over Berlin. The Mustangs began their round-trip escorts on January 5, 1944, on a mission to Kiel.

The *Luftwaffe* changed tactics again, this time to battle formations of as many as 100 aircraft, a mix of heavy types to attack the bombers and lighter types to fight the escorts. In

Rocket-armed Bf110G-2/R3s of 9/ZG 26 over Germany. (Bundesarchiv)

Loading work of Wgr. 21 mortar shell to Fw190A-7/R6. (Bundesarchiv)

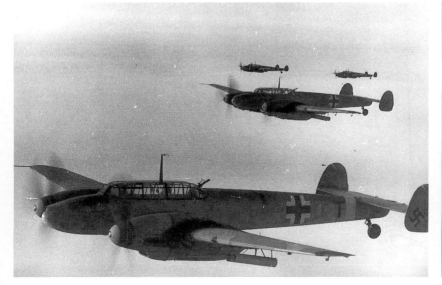

mid-1944, the first large battle units appeared in combat. They flew Fw190s, specially modified with heavier-than-standard frontal and cockpit armor, in formations against the bomber boxes. They were escorted into battle by Bf109s, assigned to cover the heavily armed—and therefore heavier and less maneuverable—Focke-Wulfs. The tactics worked; the interceptors were able to saturate the bomber defenses and often broke the box on the first pass. As many as 50 attacked at once, in closely spaced Vees of a dozen or more fighters. Designated as *Sturmgruppen*, the first unit—IV/JG3—was formed at the beginning of April 1944 and first saw action against bombers hitting Berlin on April 29.

April 1944 brought another change in the air battle, with ominous implications for the USAAF. Bomber losses to enemy anti-aircraft were 131 that month, a horrifying increase from the eight downed by flak in January. The reason: new gunlaying radars were operational with *Luftwaffe Flak* units, and *Flak* batteries were concentrated on the approaches to critical targets. The fearsome 88 mm guns were grouped in batteries of up to 24. The heavier 105 mm and 128 mm cannon also were grouped, although in smaller units. Guns were fired simultaneously on command based on radar data, and a gigantic shotgun-like blast of large-caliber shells slammed into bomber formations.

The countermove was two-fold. First, bomber box formations were altered to open the distance between individual aircraft in ways that would maintain a strong defense, but decrease vulnerability to a single large mass of exploding flak. Second, electronic countermeasures were available, and jammers known by the code name "Carpet" were carried by some of the bombers. Extensive use of "window," coupled with "Carpet" operations, countered the new flak tactics.

On July 28, 1944, a new factor was added to the interception equation: the tiny, rocket-propelled Me163. This unique interceptor was seen high above bomber formations that day, and subsequent sightings and intelligence reports confirmed its presence in German skies. On August 16, the first Me163 unit, I/JG400, made its first five sorties against the bomber streams.

On September 27, 1944, the *Sturmgruppen* had a field day, hitting the 445th BG's B-24s near Kassel. The slaughter took less than five minutes, an eternity in air combat. When it was over, 20 Liberators were down. The Germans repeated the one-sided contest the next day, shooting down 18 B-17s starting a bomb run against Magdeburg. The *Sturmgruppen* tactics had proved most effective when first used and when the mass of fighters could approach bomber formations from the rear and carry through their planned attack. But directing that mass,

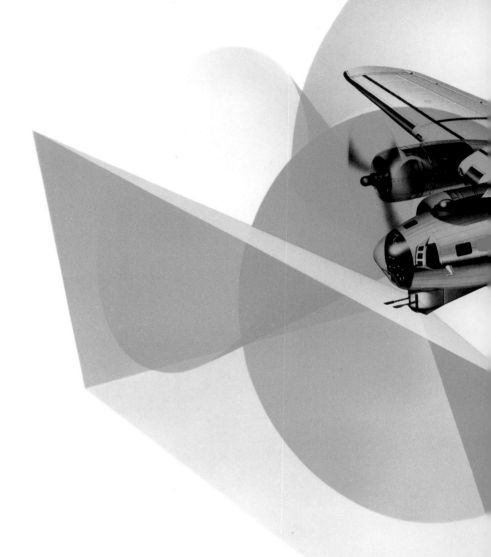

The Fw190A-8/R6 of IV/JG 3 as *Sturmgruppe* taxies with ground crew. Note the 5 mm (0.2 in) special armor plate on the outside of the cockpit. (Bundesarchiv)

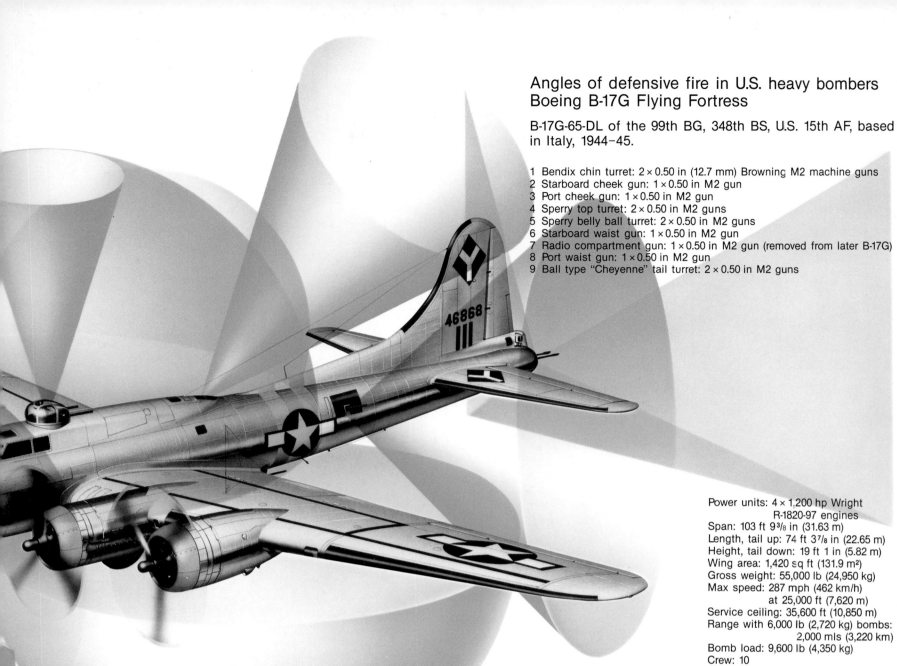

Angles of defensive fire in U.S. heavy bombers
Boeing B-17G Flying Fortress

B-17G-65-DL of the 99th BG, 348th BS, U.S. 15th AF, based in Italy, 1944–45.

1 Bendix chin turret: 2 × 0.50 in (12.7 mm) Browning M2 machine guns
2 Starboard cheek gun: 1 × 0.50 in M2 gun
3 Port cheek gun: 1 × 0.50 in M2 gun
4 Sperry top turret: 2 × 0.50 in M2 guns
5 Sperry belly ball turret: 2 × 0.50 in M2 guns
6 Starboard waist gun: 1 × 0.50 in M2 gun
7 Radio compartment gun: 1 × 0.50 in M2 gun (removed from later B-17G)
8 Port waist gun: 1 × 0.50 in M2 gun
9 Ball type "Cheyenne" tail turret: 2 × 0.50 in M2 guns

Power units: 4 × 1,200 hp Wright
R-1820-97 engines
Span: 103 ft 9³/₈ in (31.63 m)
Length, tail up: 74 ft 3⁷/₈ in (22.65 m)
Height, tail down: 19 ft 1 in (5.82 m)
Wing area: 1,420 sq ft (131.9 m²)
Gross weight: 55,000 lb (24,950 kg)
Max speed: 287 mph (462 km/h)
at 25,000 ft (7,620 m)
Service ceiling: 35,600 ft (10,850 m)
Range with 6,000 lb (2,720 kg) bombs:
2,000 mls (3,220 km)
Bomb load: 9,600 lb (4,350 kg)
Crew: 10

forming it up, and moving it around the sky were difficult, time-consuming tasks, and the Mustangs were in no mood to watch while this was going on. They bored in first and broke up the German formations time and time again.

The experimental *Kommando Nowotny* was formed at Achmer in September, equipped with 30 Messerschmitt Me262 twin-engined jet-propelled interceptors. These advanced fighters were much more of a potential threat than the Me163. With their speed and endurance, they would be able to attack bomber formations repeatedly, pulling away easily from the defending escort fighters.

But even though jet and rocket fighters could easily blow through escort screens to get at the bombers, they still had only a two-second firing pass. Closing speeds were near 700 mph (1,310 km/h), so that the Me262 pilots had to open fire sooner and break away sooner—perhaps at 1,000 yards (900 m) and 200 yards (180 m) respectively. As an alternate tactic, *Kommando Nowotny* pilots blasted through the escorts from the rear of the formation, flying at top speed (close to Mach 0.8), then dove to a position a mile behind and a quarter-mile (400 m) below the bombers. From there, they made a high-g pullup which bled off airspeed rapidly. They leveled off even with the

A *Feldwebel* instructor shows a model of B-17 for pilot training. (Bundesarchiv)

A B-17F belonged to the 94th BG, 8th AF, shot down by German fighters. (Bundesarchiv)

bombers to find themselves inside the escort screen at a relatively slow closing speed with the bombers. Then: select a target, give it a short burst, pull up, and break away.

Desperation breeds strange weapons and tactics, and tacticians with more nerve than brains decided that modified fighters could be used for suicidal attacks. The concept: get in as close as possible, protected by armor, and then open fire with heavy cannon. If that didn't work, or when ammunition was exhausted, aim the fighter so that its wing would cut through the bomber fuselage just forward of the tail and, with luck, bail out before the collision.

The chosen fighter was the Fw190A-8, equipped as for the *Sturmgruppen*. The fighter retained its standard armament of paired 13 mm MG 131 in the fuselage and four wing-mounted 20 mm MG 151/20 cannon. Frontal and cockpit armor was increased substantially.

It was tried, according to some sources, with varying degrees of success. The modification made the Fw190 a lot more robust and survivable than it had been, and so it is likely that pilots flying them were able to score more easily than before and that they were not often forced to ram. (The concept was revived in 1945 by *Sonderkommando Elbe*, flying modified Bf109G, K and Fw190A models. Its only known operation was against B-17s on April 7, and eight of the bombers lost that day were reportedly brought down by the special aircraft. But the one mission finished *Sk Elbe*; 80 percent of its aircraft never got home.)

The average *Luftwaffe* pilot—and by now, the average was neither experienced nor well-trained—was awakened at 3:00 a.m., dressed, and drove to the airfield to breakfast in the *Staffel* ready room. After eating, he went out to the flight line for a walkaround inspection of his aircraft, reporting back its readiness to the operations officer.

German radar picked up the huge bomber formations as they began to assemble over England and tracked them on the outbound leg. Typically, at about 5:30 a.m., fighters went to first-alert stage; they had to be ready to be airborne within 15 minutes after a warning of an incoming raid. The next stage was cockpit alert; pilots were helped into their parachutes and strapped in their aircraft by ground crew.

Three green rockets from a flare gun signaled the scramble. Typically, a *Gruppe* could get 50 fighters airborne in about two minutes. Pilots received instructions by radio, learn-

Consolidated B-24H Liberator

B-24H-1-FO of the 392nd BG, 578th BS, U.S. 8th AF, based at Wendling, England in 1944.

ing position, strength, altitude, and other information about the bombers, and steering instructions. When they spotted the bombers, they climbed to about 1,000 yards (900 m) above and two miles (3.2 km) in front of the bombers and dove to the attack. The trick was to get the bombers before their escorts could get the *Luftwaffe* pilots.

Individual attackers made shallow dives, opened fire, and broke over the top of the formation, pulling up into a chandelle and getting into position for another firing run. Often they

The Bf110G-2/R4 fitted with a 37 mm BK 3.7 cannon (*Flak* 18) beneath the Fuselage against USAAF heavy bombers. (Bundesarchiv)

A Bf109G-14/R1 of II/JG 3 carrying a 250 kg (551 lb) SC250 bomb with clockwork time fuze for air-to-air bombing. (Bundesarchiv)

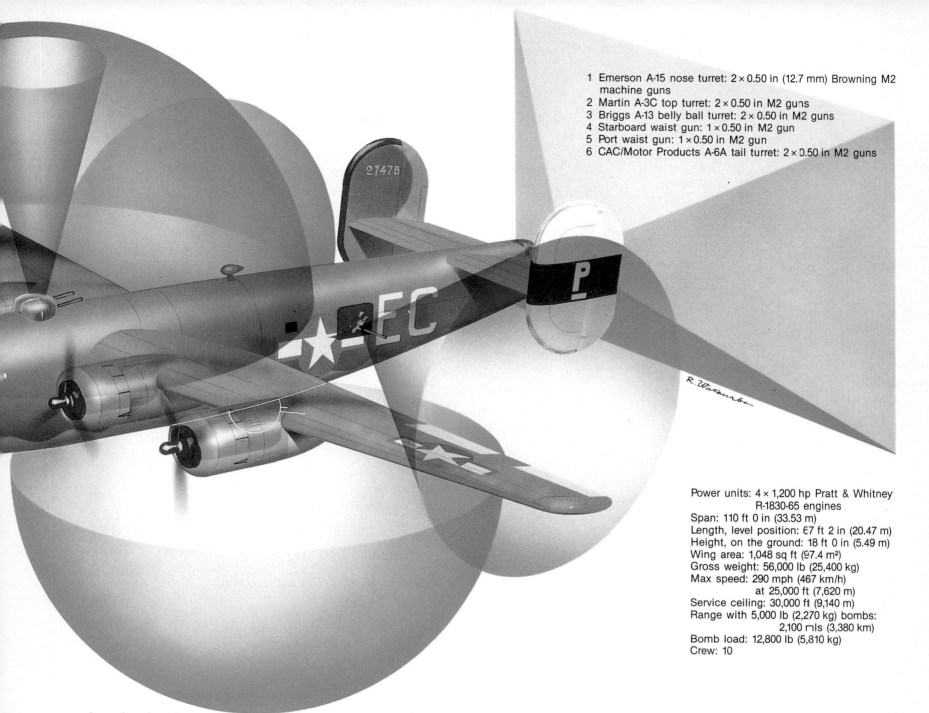

1 Emerson A-15 nose turret: 2 × 0.50 in (12.7 mm) Browning M2 machine guns
2 Martin A-3C top turret: 2 × 0.50 in M2 guns
3 Briggs A-13 belly ball turret: 2 × 0.50 in M2 guns
4 Starboard waist gun: 1 × 0.50 in M2 gun
5 Port waist gun: 1 × 0.50 in M2 gun
6 CAC/Motor Products A-6A tail turret: 2 × 0.50 in M2 guns

Power units: 4 × 1,200 hp Pratt & Whitney R-1830-65 engines
Span: 110 ft 0 in (33.53 m)
Length, level position: 67 ft 2 in (20.47 m)
Height, on the ground: 18 ft 0 in (5.49 m)
Wing area: 1,048 sq ft (97.4 m²)
Gross weight: 56,000 lb (25,400 kg)
Max speed: 290 mph (467 km/h) at 25,000 ft (7,620 m)
Service ceiling: 30,000 ft (9,140 m)
Range with 5,000 lb (2,270 kg) bombs: 2,100 mls (3,380 km)
Bomb load: 12,800 lb (5,810 kg)
Crew: 10

were forced to break to the sides or below, or were attacked on the pullup, and the rules changed, as they do continually in the fluid maelstrom of air combat.

The contest between heavy bombers and daylight interceptors, as played out over Germany, was in the end a very uneven one. German tactics were simply not able to change rapidly enough, or to be effective enough, to drive away any of the daylight raids. New weapons were introduced without waiting to mass them for a really staggering blow. The *Luftwaffe* never really saw the problem; its concentration was on shooting down bombers. The escorts hardly ever were intercepted in their own right, but only when they were in the way of an attack on the bombers. And the *Luftwaffe* never tried to hit the many bases of the Eighth AF or to disrupt their operations while they were still over England.

For those, and other reasons, the *Luftwaffe* lost its daylight war in the air against the heavy bombers of the USAAF.

A veteran fighter pilot teaches head-on attack against heavy-armed B-24 bomber to young trainees. (Bundesarchiv)

A shot down B-24 Liberator of the 8th AF. The *Luftwaffe* made use of these captured aircraft for research. (Bundesarchiv)

Airborne Radar Joins the Battle

In Germany and Great Britain, night interceptors were part of a defense system that included ground-based radars, unmodified day fighters, searchlights, barrage balloons, and anti-aircraft artillery, augmented by occasional short-term employment of unusual weapons like unguided rockets. Ground-based radars detected and defined targets; ground controllers interpreted the radar returns and passed intercept data to fighters by radio. Fighter pilots followed those instructions and flew toward an intercept point somewhere in the blackness. In theory, the system directed the fighter within visual detection range of his quarry; in practice, the radars were not accurate enough to do that consistently.

The gap between the hunter and the hunted had to be closed, or at least reduced, by other means. Airborne radar equipment was the solution to the problem, and all the warring powers made great efforts to develop lightweight, reliable, and accurate airborne radar systems.

The advent of airborne radar systems for detection, tracking, and approaching targets is the arbitrary dividing line chosen in this book to separate two categories of night interception. Chapter 3 described night interceptions made possible by human eyes; this chapter will describe some aspects of British and German night interception systems using the artificial electronic eyes of airborne radar.

When Royal Air Force Fighter Command first faced the German onslaught in the Battle of Britain that began in mid-August 1940, the aircraft at its disposal were preponderantly day fighters. The Command's strength included 30 squadrons of Hurricanes, 19 of Spitfires, and a few squadrons of obsolescent biplane Gladiators. Neither those aircraft nor their airfields were equipped for night flying, let alone night fighting, and few of the pilots had any night-flying experience. Yet they were expected—in fact, ordered—to intercept German bombers by night.

Ground-based radars existed, and air interception (AI) radars were in development. In fact, a few early AI sets had become available and had been installed in a handful of twin-engined long-range Bristol Blenheim IF day fighters, modifying them to rudimentary night-fighter configuration. Deliveries had begun to RAF squadrons at the end of July 1939. The RAF Fighter Interception Unit (FIU), a developmental and operational testing establishment, began using Blenheims operationally in November 1939.

As with most primitive new equipment, reliability and performance both were low, and the results of attempted interceptions continued to be disappointing. But on the night of July 22, 1940, a Blenheim maneuvered into position behind a Dornier Do17 and blew it out of the sky.

The RAF had eight squadrons assigned to night-fighting duties to defend the British Isles against the German medium bomber night offensive—called "The Blitz" by most of those who experienced the bombing—that began in September 1940, after the Battle of Britain had been won. None of the RAF night-fighting aircraft had been designed originally for that mission, and most were barely capable of safe and efficient night flight. Six squadrons were equipped with Blenheim IF fighters, some aircraft with AI radar with a minimum operating range of 800 ft (240 m) and a maximum of two miles (3.2 km). The other two squadrons flew Boulton-Paul Defiant fighters, transferred to the force because they were useless as day fighters.

British ground-based radars, although capable of detecting aircraft out to 100 miles (160 km) or more over water, lacked the precision to track aircraft paths with high accuracy. They could not consistently direct night fighters close enough to their targets so that the fighters' radar could be used to close the gap, although that was the hope that led to the development of AI radar in the first place.

Consequently, early operations of British fighters against German bombers were conducted by combining ground radar indications with visual observations by the fighters (popularly called "cat's eyes" tactics by public and RAF alike), and additionally hoping for good luck. Those operations were confined primarily to moonlit nights. In bad weather, or above fog, mists, and cloud cover, the German bomber crews had a free ride, guided to their targets by an ingenious system of electronic navigational aids.

But a number of things were happening almost simultaneously that would eventually coalesce into an effective air defense of the British Isles by night. One was the well-known radar chain along the coasts of England, covering the inbound approaches that German bombers would use. Another was the development of the early form of identification and positioning equipment called "Pip-Squeak." Third was a grid of ground-based radar beacons to assist a night-fighter pilot in establishing his position over England. Fourth was the arrival of the VHF (Very High Frequency) voice radio system.

To this quartet of supporting measures should be added a fifth, and primary, weapon: The Bristol Beaufighter. Blunt, strong, with high performance, the Beau was the ideal candidate for night fighting. It had twin wing-mounted engines, leaving the fuselage nose clear for the installation of a radar system. It had performance to catch anything the Germans could put into the sky. And it mounted four 20 mm Hispano automatic cannon in its belly, with additional firepower from six .303-cal (7.7 mm) machine guns in its wings. It first flew in July 1939 and was working with the FIU a little more than a year later. By September 1940, it armed four night-fighter squadrons and was equipped with AI Mark IV radar that could track enemy aircraft at ranges between 400 feet (120 m) and three miles (4.8 km).

And it was needed desperately. During the German assault of more than 12,000 sorties against London between September 7 and November 13, 1940, the *Luftwaffe* dropped 13,000 tons of high explosives and about a million incendiary bombs. More than 13,000 Londoners were killed, 20,000 injured. The Germans lost 81 aircraft to the air defense system, 54 of them to anti-aircraft guns, four to barrage balloons, and only eight to fighters. Coming after the outstanding record of Fighter Command during the Battle of Britain, these very light German losses were a source of deep frustration and a severe blow to the spirits of the pilots.

On November 14, the bombers changed their targets from London to the cities of the Midlands, hammering Coventry in a raid that has since become an archetype of conventional bombing. The Germans completely ruled the sky that night, pounding the city and the six industrial targets that had been singled out. No British aircraft intercepted or destroyed any

No. 600 Squadron's Bristol Beaufighter Mk IFs equipped with AI Mk IV radars. Photographed on May 23, 1941. (Imperial War Museum)

German bomber. Five nights later an RAF Beaufighter finally scored a first kill, downing a Junkers Ju88.

Abortive attempts to develop effective weapons included the Large Aerial Mine (LAM), a small explosive charge attached to one end of a 2,000 ft (610 m) cable and a parachute attached to the other. These were to be dropped from—presumably—patrolling aircraft in a group across the path of incoming bombers. When a bomber hit the wires, the drag of the chute would pull the charge up to the airplane's wing, where it would explode. This idea was developed and deployed with an operational squadron, cost untold amounts of money and effort, placed British aircraft crews at risk, and was totally useless.

The Turbinlite system, another attempt, required a three-plane team. The lead aircraft was an American-built twin-engined Douglas Havoc light bomber with a pushed-in, flattened nose that mounted a large searchlight and radar antennas. A single Hurricane fighter flew on each flank of the Havoc. The team was vectored to the approximate location of enemy aircraft, and when the Havoc operator was certain of his target, the searchlight was turned on. The Hurricanes then were to shoot the enemy down.

This scheme was doomed to fail, because it tacitly assumed—as so often happens in many new weapons concepts—that the enemy would cooperate by flying straight and level. Instead, the instant the searchlight went on, the enemy pilot took violent evasive action and was immediately lost in the blackness. The brilliant glare of the Turbinlite destroyed whatever night vision accommodation the Hurricane pilots had developed, and they were useless for the next few minutes as they tried to avoid collision with each other and with the Havoc. The Turbinlite system finally did manage to score once, shooting down an RAF aircraft.

While these projects were underway, scientists had been developing a new radar system for overland tracking. The Chain Home system worked well but was aimed out to sea and was useless once incoming invaders crossed the coast. The first new radar became operational in October 1940 and was able to track aircraft out to about 45 miles (72 km). Further, it plotted the returns on a Plan Position Indicator (PPI) scope, showing the bomber, any intercepting fighters, and characteristics of the terrain underneath. The accuracy was good enough to direct intercept as close as 3,000 feet (910 m); the fighter's radar was powerful enough to take it from there.

By the spring of 1941, five of the six original Blenheim squadrons had re-equipped with new Beaufighters with AI Mark IV, now standard for RAF night fighters. Nearly a dozen ground-controlled intercept (GCI) stations were operational, and the night defense system was rapidly gaining on the German attackers. The toll of bombers, which had measured three and four in January and February, rose to 22 in March, 48 in April, and 96 in May. March was the first month in which aircraft had downed more bombers at night than had anti-aircraft guns. The April scoreboard read 48 for the fighters and 39 for the guns. May was even better; 96 bombers downed by night fighters, 31 by guns.

Analysis of the increasing numbers of victories showed that they were divided about equally between radar-equipped fighters and visual intercepts by the "cat's eyes," but the key factor was that radar-equipped fighters made twice as many contacts in half the number of sorties. That factor decided the course of the RAF. AI radar and GCI was to be the future.

But by then, the Blitz was running out of steam. Hitler had decided to invade Russia, and every unit was being drained or repositioned for the coming attack. As a result, *Luftwaffe*

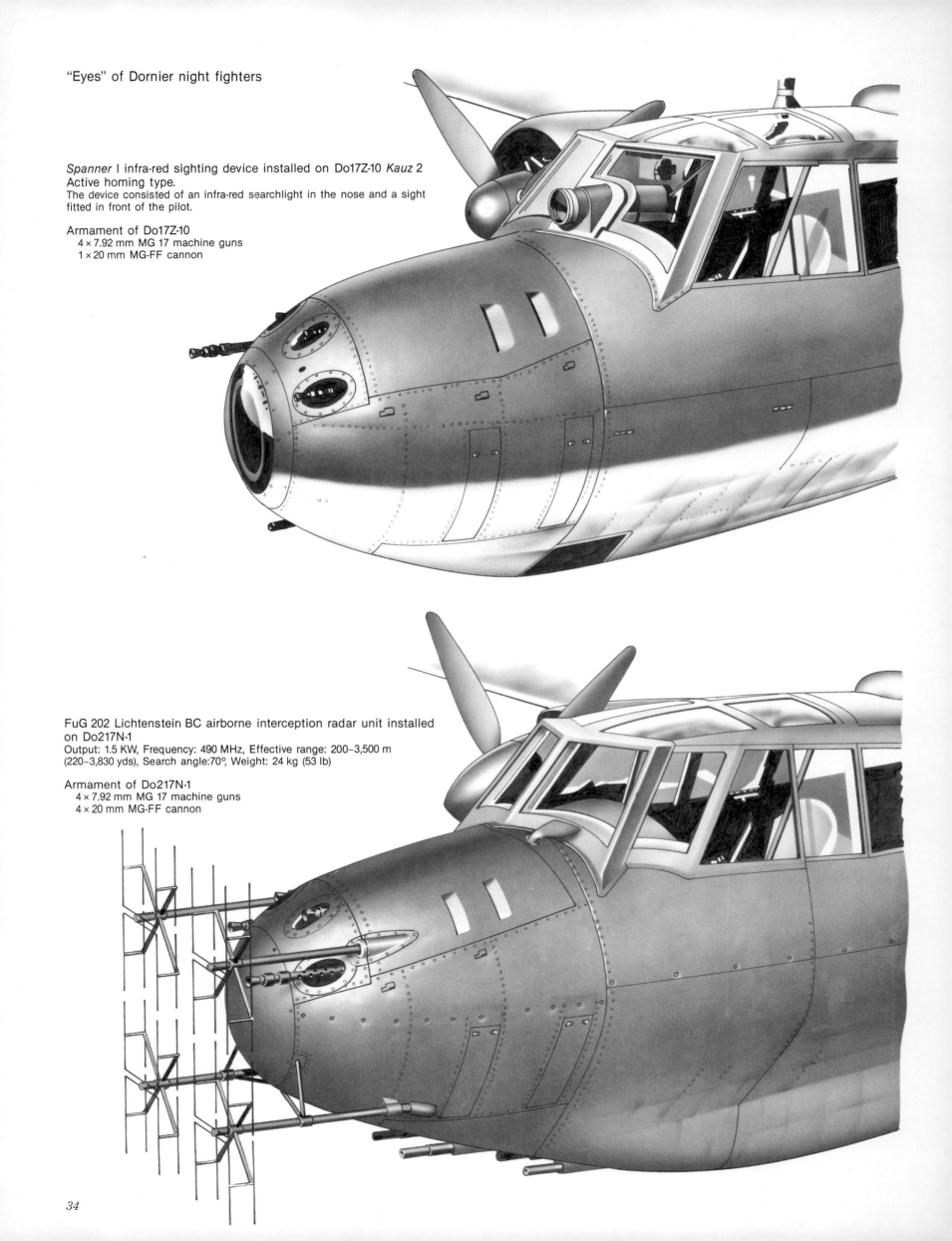

"Eyes" of Dornier night fighters

Spanner I infra-red sighting device installed on Do17Z-10 *Kauz* 2
Active homing type.
The device consisted of an infra-red searchlight in the nose and a sight
fitted in front of the pilot.

Armament of Do17Z-10
   4 × 7.92 mm MG 17 machine guns
   1 × 20 mm MG-FF cannon

FuG 202 Lichtenstein BC airborne interception radar unit installed
on Do217N-1
Output: 1.5 KW, Frequency: 490 MHz, Effective range: 200–3,500 m
(220–3,830 yds), Search angle:70°, Weight: 24 kg (53 lb)

Armament of Do217N-1
   4 × 7.92 mm MG 17 machine guns
   4 × 20 mm MG-FF cannon

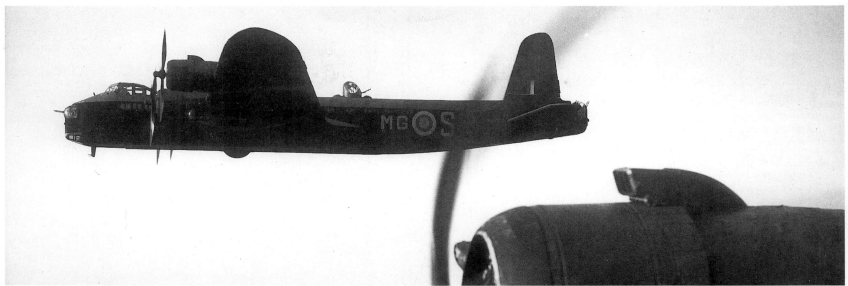

Short Stirling Mk Is belonged to No. 7 Squadron in flight. The Stirling was the first of three four-engined heavy bombers to enter service in RAF Bomber Command. (Imperial War Museum)

strength moved from the Western front to the East, and Britain was never again threatened by any substantial force of night—or day—raiders.

Airborne radar developments in Germany had preceded the war, and so, by the middle of 1941, the first AI unit was ready for *Luftwaffe* service. Designated FuG (*Funkgerät* = radio apparatus) 202 and code-named *Lichtenstein* B/C, it had a working range between 200 and 3,500 m (660 to 11,500 ft). The first recorded intercept using the new equipment occurred the night of August 9/10, 1941. A twin-engined Do215B-5, with FuG202 antennas bristling from its nose, lifted off the airfield at Leeuwarden in the Netherlands and bored up into the night. Its crew soon detected a bomber, approached from the rear, and shot it down.

At that time, German night fighter operations were still tied to the zoned system developed by Kammhuber. There was no sophisticated method of ground control that could hand over data from zone to zone, enabling a single coordinated mass attack against a bomber onslaught. And whatever radar guidance German ground units could provide was completely neutralized by the RAF use of "window," first dropped during the July 24/25 night raid on Hamburg in 1943. The Germans increased flak concentrations, used gun-laying radars, added radar to searchlights, increased the number of searchlights. But the kill rate still lagged far below what was needed to make night trips over Germany impossible for the RAF.

Further, the British began to plan their attacks for nights of bad weather, making things difficult for the Wild Boar pilots, whose day fighters had not been equipped for operations at night. Night fighting was still a visual experience acted out

against a backdrop of bright lights. Wild Boar pilots often couldn't find their home airfields, often lacked the training, flying skills, and equipment to approach in bad weather even if they could locate their field, and too frequently crashed on landing.

The Wild Boar experiment, though only a stop-gap solution, gave breathing time to tacticians and radar specialists to concentrate on controlled night interception techniques and to augment aircraft with an increasing variety of airborne radar and radio installations of higher and higher performance and quality.

Remember, though, that electronic devices of the time were built around tubes rather than transistors. The equipment was bulky and heavy; further, tubes were sensitive to the shattering vibrations of nearby cannon fire. Consequently, however strong in numbers the *Luftwaffe* night fighters were, the actual availability of aircraft to be dispatched on missions was only a fraction—perhaps a third, at best—of a unit's strength.

The Germans, as the British had, concentrated their night-fighter efforts on twin-engined multi-place aircraft like the Bf110. That obsolescent airplane, once proudly called a "destroyer," proved to be an excellent night fighter. It could carry the weapons and electronics required, was fairly simple and easy to fly, and was produced in enormous quantities.

Three other twin-engined aircraft were developed as excellent night fighters: the Junkers Ju88, Dornier Do215, and Dornier Do217 series. Each of these, along with the Bf110, was produced in a number of sub-models with changes in equipment, powerplant, and weapons. Near the end of the war, a handful of other aircraft types—the Heinkel He219, Focke-Wulf

A Bf110G-4/R1 of 9/NJG 3 fitted with FuG 202 *Lichtenstein* BC radar on a daylight operation in the summer of 1943. (Bundesarchiv)

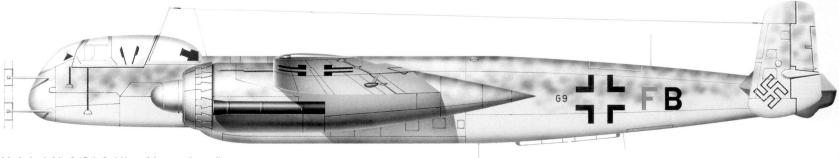

Heinkel He219A-0 *Uhu* (Horned owl)

flown by *Major* Werner Streib, *Kommandeur* of I/NJG 1. The aircraft was wrecked on landing after destroying five RAF heavy bombers on the night of June 11–12, 1943.

Power units
2 × Daimler-Benz DB603A 12-cylinder liquid-cooled engines:
   1,750 hp each for take-off
   1,850 hp each at 2,100 m (6,890 ft)
Dimensions
   Span: 18.50 m (60 ft 8³⁄₈ in)
   Length, level position, without radar aerials: 15.54 m (50 ft 11¹³⁄₁₆ in)
   Height: 4.10 m (13 ft 5⁷⁄₁₆ in)
   Wing area: 44.5 m² (479 sq ft)

Weights (A-5/R2, about the same as A-O)
   Empty: 9,900 kg (21,830 lb)
   Gross: 13,150 kg (28,990 lb)
Performance
   Max speed: 560 km/h (348 mph) at 5,700 m (18,700 ft)
   Time to climb to 6,000 m (19,690 ft): 11.5 min
   Service ceiling: 9,300 m (30,510 ft)
   Range: 2,100 km (1,305 mls)
Armament
   2 × 30 mm Mk 108 cannon
   4 × 20 mm MG 151/20 cannon
Crew 2

Ta154, Arado Ar234, and Messerschmitt Me262—became operational, but were held to few sorties and victories because of fuel shortages or unreliability of equipment. Some of these types were not intended to be night hunters of heavy bombers, but were designed to intercept and attack enemy night-fighters and high-altitude reconnaissance aircraft.

The later model interceptors carried upgraded radars that operated at shorter wavelengths than the early equipment. Probably the greatest failure in the German radar effort was the continuing reliance on the early equipment simply because it was in full-scale production. Scientific establishments neglected the shorter-wave, higher-frequency radar systems until too late in the war, and as a result, the British were able to jam and disrupt at will almost every piece of airborne and ground electronic equipment the Germans used. On D-Day, for example, the British jammed every ground radar within miles of the invasion site. The Germans were unable to get a single night fighter into the air over the beaches.

Jamming was an essential part of night interception. Electronic warfare, with its countermeasures and counter-countermeasures, was just becoming the silent partner of fighting forces, and "window" was only the beginning of that phase of war. Between its introduction and the end of the conflict, British and German ingenuity produced devices to interfere, jam, and disrupt radars and radio. Both sides also developed counters to those countermeasures, a common one being a device that homed on a jammer, so that the aircraft interfering

with a search radar could be found and shot down.

"Window" jammed everything, impartially, that operated in the high-frequency radio wavelengths then standard for most equipment. *Lichtenstein* BC and FuG212 *Lichtenstein* C-1 was no exception. But an improved model, FuG220 *Lichtenstein* SN-2, operated on a longer wavelength as yet unjammed by the British, and its availability began to turn the tide.

German ground controllers introduced a technique known as the "running commentary," continuous verbal data, transmitted by radio to the night fighters, identifying the strength and locations of bomber formations. (The British succeeded in cutting into the running commentary and issued countermanding orders, spoken in perfect German, frustrating

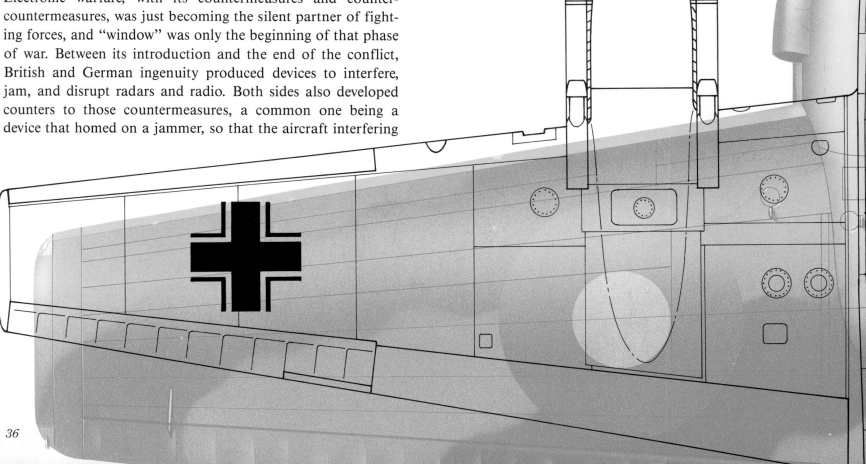

both German controllers and pilots.) In new tactics—*Zahme Sau* (Tame Boar)—night fighters were dispatched to a holding area over a beacon, then directed to intercept and join the bomber stream from there. Once in among the bombers, the night fighters transmitted direction-finding data automatically. Other night fighters homed on those signals, joined the stream, and began to kill bombers.

In spite of the effective British disruption of communications and radars, Bomber Command achieved only a temporary control of the air over Germany. German ground controllers learned to tell real bombers from spurious returns caused by clouds of "window." Both Wild Boar and Tame Boar tactics were producing kills. Bomber losses began to climb, reaching high levels in March 1944. And another reason for the increase in night-fighter successes was a clever adaptation of aircraft cannon in a project that received the nickname of "*Schräge Musik*" (jazz): the installation of a pair of 20 mm MG-FF cannon mounted behind the pilot to fire obliquely upward and forward.

German night fighters had first used "*Schräge Musik*" the night of August 17, 1943, during the heavy RAF raid on Peenemünde to shoot down six bombers whose crews never knew what hit them. Before then, night fighters approached

Handley Page Halifax B Mk II Series I

Power units: 4 × 1,390 hp Rolls-Royce
          Merlin XX engines
Span: 98 ft 8 in (30.07 m)
Length, tail up: 69 ft 9 in (21.26 m)
Height, tail down, over D/F loop:
          20 ft 9 in (6.32 m)
Wing area: 1,200 sq ft (111.5 m²)
Gross weight: 51,500 lb (23,360 kg)
Max speed: 261 mph (420 km/h)
          at 19,500 ft (5,940 m)
Service ceiling: 22,000 ft (6,710 m)
Range with 6,500 lb (2,950 kg) bombs:
          1,900 mls (3,060 km)
Bomb load: 13,000 lb (5,900 kg)
Defensive fire: 8 × 0.303 in (7.7 mm)
          machine guns
Crew: 6–7

Messerschmitt Bf110G-4

Power units: 2 × 1,475 hp Daimler-Benz
          DB605B-1 engines
Span: 16.25 m (53 ft 3⁷/₉ in)
Length, without radar antennas:
          12.07 m (39 ft 7³/₁₆ in)
Height: 4.18 m (13 ft 8⁹/₁₆ in)
Wing area: 38.4 m² (413.4 sq ft)
Gross weight: 9,300 kg (20,500 lb)
Max speed: approx. 500 km/h (310 mph)
Service ceiling: 8,000 m (26,250 ft)
Armament: 2 × 20 mm MG 151/20
          cannon
          4 × 7.92 mm MG 17
          machine guns
          1 × MG 81Z
          (2 × 7.92 mm machine guns)
Crew: 3

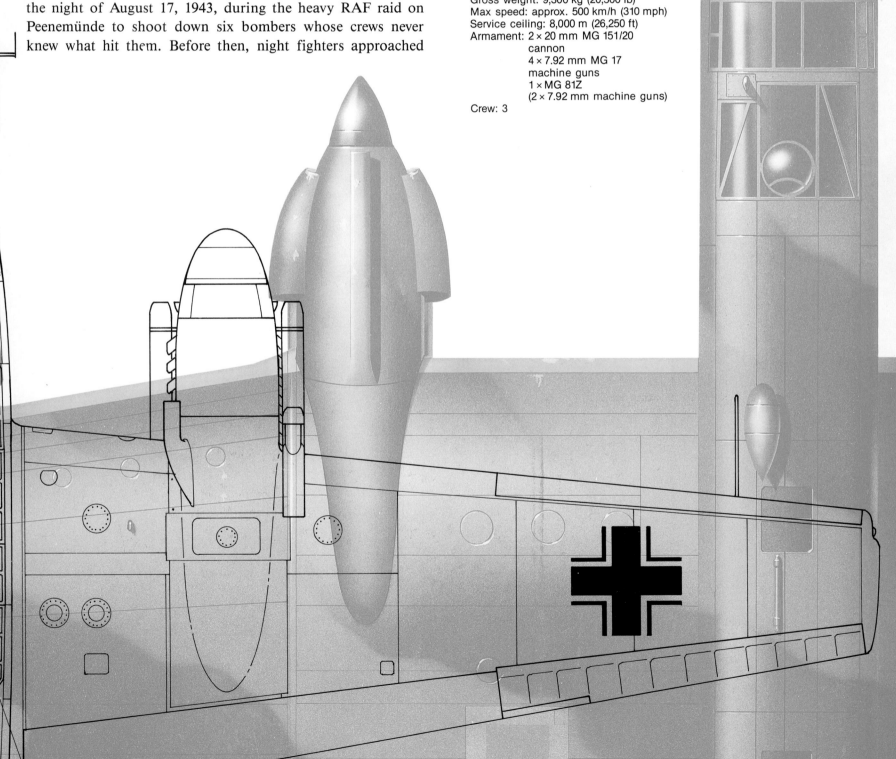

The heavily burnt wreckage of Avro Lancaster downed by German night fighter in 1943. (Bundesarchiv)

The F.N.20 tail turret carried four 0.303 in (7.7 mm) machine guns on a Lancaster. (Imperial War Museum)

their targets from behind and below, then pulled up to fire, hoping that they would be close enough to shoot and kill from that vulnerable position before the bomber's tail gunner did so first. With the obliquely firing cannon, the night fighter still approached from behind and below the bomber, but flew a level course, gradually overhauling his target and establishing a position underneath. Then the crew used the sighting equipment that was part of the *"Schräge Musik"* installation, aiming at the wing center section of the dark bulk overhead or between engines well-defined by exhaust flames.

Following initial successes with a few field installations of *"Schräge Musik,"* other night-fighter units demanded the installations, and it eventually became a production standard on late models of Bf110 and other night fighters. RAF bomber losses began to rise dramatically. And, said the official history, "Bomber Command was compelled, largely by the German night fighter force, to draw away from its primary target, Berlin...The Battle of Berlin was more than a failure. It was a defeat."

The German night fighter forces regained control of the skies over Germany in three fierce and decisive air battles. February 19, 1944, the RAF targeted Leipzig with 823 bombers

and lost 78. March 24, against Berlin, 72 were shot down. And the frightful Nürnberg raid of March 30 was the final blow. On that clear and moonlit night, when any bomber force, regardless of strength, should have stayed on the ground, Bomber Command mounted a thousand-plane raid that slammed into a hornet's nest.

The incoming bombers took a route that placed them within the reach of every single night-fighter unit the *Luftwaffe* had. Bomber Command dispatched 999 aircraft, 832 of which went to the target and returned to base. They left behind 97 bombers, 79 of them downed by night fighters. The *Luftwaffe* lost 11 men; the RAF, 545.

The *Luftwaffe* Tame Boar tactics worked overtime. The fighters orbited a beacon that placed them practically in the path of the incoming bomber stream. At one point, the German night fighters were destroying a British bomber each minute. Bomber pilots counted dozens of burning aircraft along their route. On that night, the *Luftwaffe* dispatched 246 sorties, claiming 101 bombers destroyed and another six probably destroyed. Postwar research showed those figures to be exaggerated by nearly a third; battle claims invariably were higher than actual losses.

Bf110G-4/R3s of 7/NJG 4 fitted with new FuG 220 *Lichtenstein* SN-2 radar sets in 1944. Note 300 ltr (79 U.S. gal) drop tanks for the long range-mission under the wings. (Bundesarchiv)

High efficiency radar-equipped de Havilland Mosquito NF 19 about to take off on a bomber-escort operation. (Imperial War Museum)

Bomber Command lost 12 percent of its force on the Nürnberg raid; coming on the heels of higher-than-expected losses over Leipzig and Berlin, Bomber Command's night air offensive against Germany was stopped in its tracks.

The zenith of German nighttime interceptions of heavy bombers was reached between November 18, 1943, (start of the Battle of Berlin) and March 30, 1944 (the Nürnberg raid). During that time, Bomber Command mounted 35 major strikes against German cities. Night interceptions accounted for most of the 1,047 bombers lost and the 1,682 damaged in those 18 cruel weeks of attack and interception.

The Germans discovered early during the British night offensive that the bombers were carrying powerful radar (known to the British by its nickname, H2S) as a navigation and bombing aid. H2S transmitted a signal that was reflected by the terrain below, received, and processed on board to produce a map of the countryside on a cockpit display. But any signal transmitted can be received and, if received from two or more locations, can be plotted. The Germans did this with great success. They were able to track British bombers from the time they turned on their radars at takeoff until they shut them down after returning to base. The bomber streams trailed a telltale track that could be read for miles.

The same mistake was made with the first tail-warning radar the British used. It was coded "Monica," and it, too, was an active transmitter that sent out bursts of radar energy to detect any aircraft within a 45-degree cone extending rearward out to 1,000 yards (900 m). Its transmissions became an input for a passive homing system, the FuG227 *Flensburg*, that could detect a Monica in operation at a range up to 60 miles (100 km).

The final statistics of German nighttime interceptions are impressive. Between 1940, when they first scored, until the end of the war, *Luftwaffe* night fighters claimed a total of 5,730 aircraft destroyed, primarily four-engined, multi-place heavy bombers. In the last days of the war, the well-equipped night interceptor carried AI radar, a precision radio altimeter, tail-warning radar, homing devices that tracked enemy jammers, IFF (Identification, Friend or Foe) gear, and integrating cockpit displays. It was armed with heavy-caliber cannon in paired installations of four or six.

That formula represents the basic design criteria for modern fighters. The World War II battles for the skies at night decided the design of subsequent generations of fighters.

Major Wilhelm Herget, *Kommandeur* of I/NJG 4, sits in the Bf110G-4/R3 pilot's seat. He scored 57 night victories until the end of the War. (Bundesarchiv)

Ground crew check the equipment of NJG 4's Bf110G-4/R3. Two *Schräge Musik* cannon are seen in the gunner's cockpit. (Bundesarchiv)

Japanese fighter pilots called the B-17E heavy bomber "the impregnability" during the early stage of the war. (Boeing)

Setting Sun, Rising Bomber

If a historian should wish to study an ineffectual air defense system, he or she will find the archetype in Japan during World War II. What is so remarkable, in retrospect, is the success the Japanese defense forces did have and the fear they engendered. Both are out of all proportion to the original investment in time and money.

The inefficiency had its roots in the Japanese military psyche, which was based on the concept of the offensive and the attack. Defeat was a personal, a national disgrace, and unthinkable. So Japanese military commanders would not, or could not, consider defeat. Japanese pilots, as well as other members of the armed forces, were expected to attack every time.

There were other factors. The Japanese Army and Navy were fiercely and blindly competitive and had no established routine for trading or sharing information. There never was a unified Japanese air defense command, even when the islands were being fire-bombed and there was every prospect of invasion. But there were, finally, air defense commands organized by both Army and Navy.

What physical defenses the country managed to establish were weak (although bomber crews attacking Japan late in the war would argue that point fiercely). By December 1941, the Army had emplaced 458 anti-aircraft guns to defend 39 key cities and had assigned 133 aircraft (118 fighters and 15 reconnaissance aircraft) to the home-defense mission. The Navy deployed 210 AA guns to protect nine harbor areas and had designated 122 fighters for air defense. A large number of the pilots assigned were junior and inexperienced.

Air defense, as with every other branch of the Japanese air forces, suffered severely because of a chronic neglect of logistics. Warriors didn't want to be in command of a warehouse of spare parts. Logistic supply had a very low priority among the Japanese forces, and one can only marvel at the ingenuity of the mechanics, themselves regarded with little respect, who managed to keep Japanese aircraft airborne and fighting.

The Japanese and Germans didn't communicate effectively with each other either. German radar developments, for example, never were widely accepted by the Japanese military. The result: Japan fought without airborne radar systems until 1943, and then had inferior equipment. (In 1928, a Japanese scientist had done the first laboratory work on microwave radar, practically a generation ahead of the rest of the world. And Professor Yagi's radar receiving antenna concept now is a

familiar sight; it's the television antenna that tops millions of houses around the world. He accomplished that work before 1930. Ironically, U.S. Navy aircraft used the Yagi antenna to aid combat in the Pacific long before the Japanese did.)

Japanese air arms never made any coordinated use of airborne radar, although some airplanes carried it near the end of the war. Japanese radio communications have been described by one authority as "chaotic," and interceptions never were directed by ground-based radar operators.

And as good as Japanese fighters were in air-to-air combat, their performance in an air-defense mission left much to be desired. They were at their best only at medium altitudes, generally below 6,000 m (19,700 ft); above that, they were not as maneuverable, and their engine power decreased sharply.

Japanese documentation of their side of the war is sparse. On the American side, reports of Japanese tactics reach no further back than the immediate attack of a fighter against a bomber or other fighter. Consequently, most American combat reports and documentary studies go no deeper than "Japanese fighters bounced us over the target." What stands out in post-action reports is the exception, rather than the rule: the lone fighter who rammed a B-17 or the three who dive-bombed a formation of B-24s.

During the first few months of the war, USAAF intelligence teams analyzed hundreds of combat reports, trying to determine a pattern to Japanese interception tactics. The findings were issued in reports circulated to USAAF units. They are a basic source for this chapter.

When the U.S. went to war, there were about 35 B-17C and D models available in the Philippines. The force was reduced rapidly; 14 were able to leave the islands for refuge in Australia; 11 of them left Darwin in a move to Java, and only three returned. That force was defensively weak, anyway, designed and developed on the accepted truth that bombers were so fast and so well-defended that they would be rarely attacked.

Units operating the B-17D bombed from altitudes between 22,000 and 30,000 ft (6,700 and 9,100 m), generally in a formation of three-plane Vees. They were attacked by Japanese fighters, who approached in a mass, then broke to dive from above or climb from below the tail. Most attackers fired and then turned away in a steep climb difficult for gunners to follow. (The B-17D had hand-operated .50-cal (12.7 mm) guns in the upper and lower rear fuselage, and at waist positions.) Bomber pilots under attack used the rudder to swing the bomber from side to side so that the waist guns could get a shot at attackers coming in from the tail. Beam attacks were not

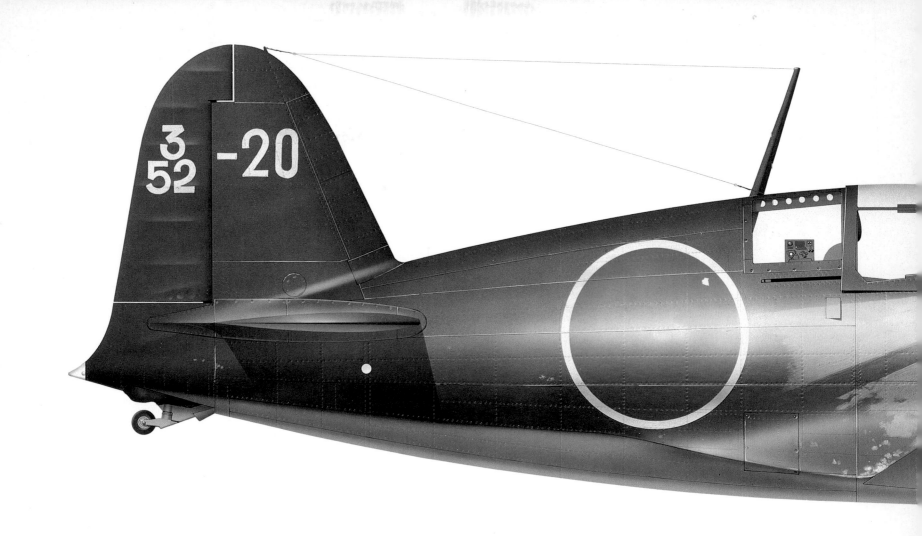

Japanese Navy Interceptors

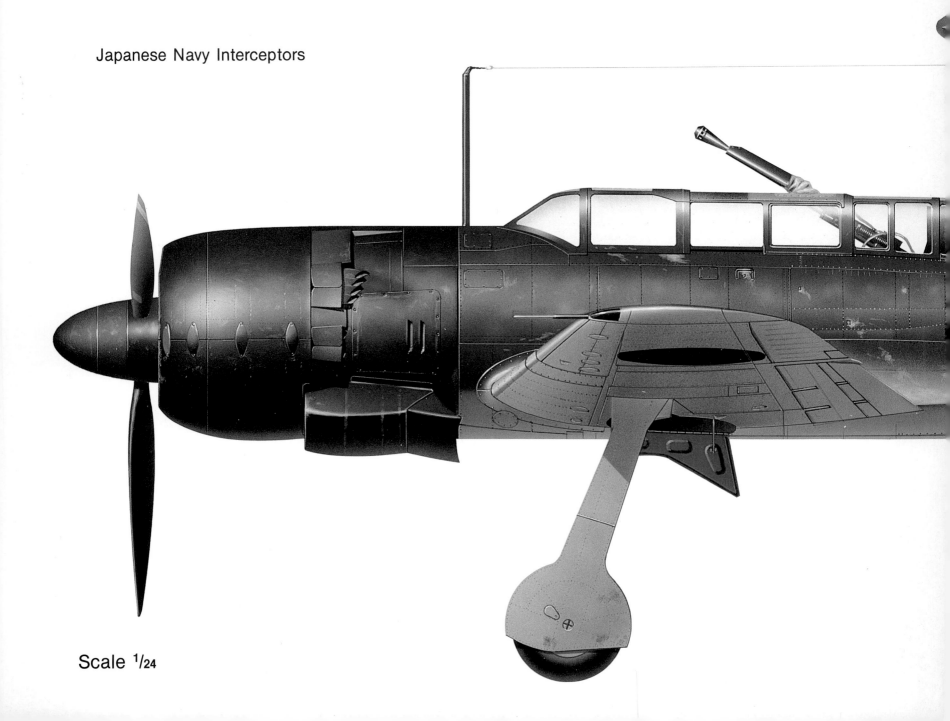

Scale ¹/₂₄

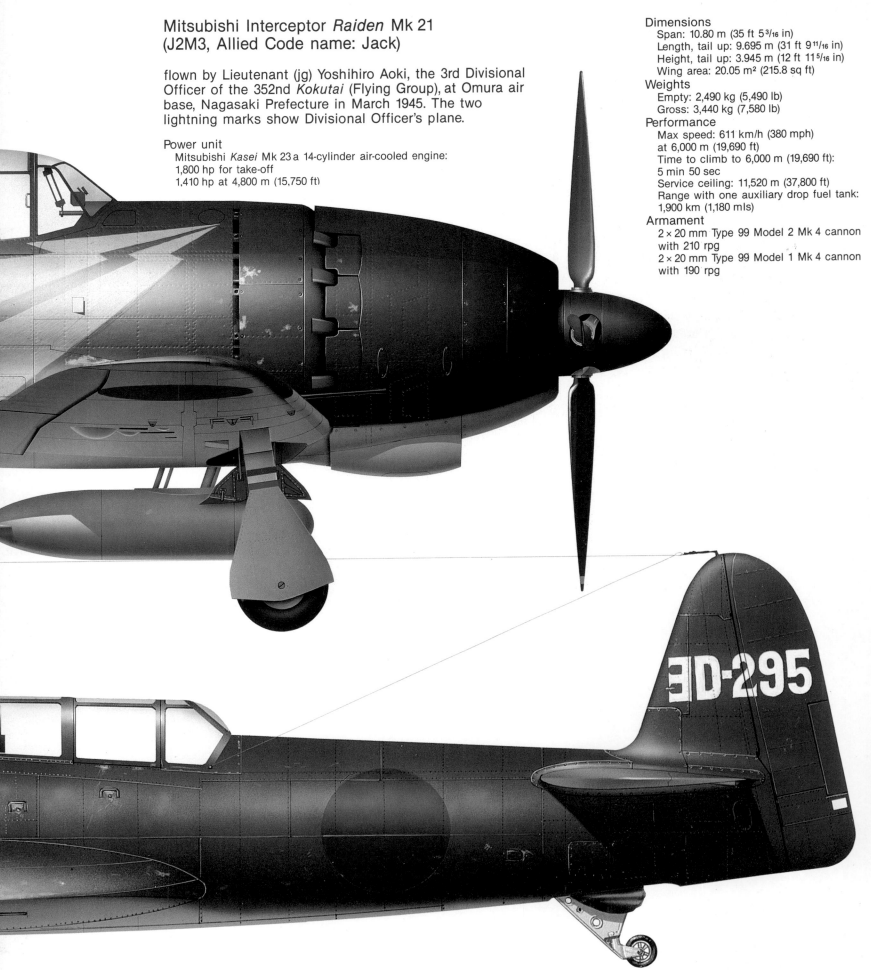

Mitsubishi Interceptor *Raiden* Mk 21
(J2M3, Allied Code name: Jack)

flown by Lieutenant (jg) Yoshihiro Aoki, the 3rd Divisional Officer of the 352nd *Kokutai* (Flying Group), at Omura air base, Nagasaki Prefecture in March 1945. The two lightning marks show Divisional Officer's plane.

Power unit
Mitsubishi *Kasei* Mk 23 a 14-cylinder air-cooled engine:
1,800 hp for take-off
1,410 hp at 4,800 m (15,750 ft)

Dimensions
Span: 10.80 m (35 ft 5 3/16 in)
Length, tail up: 9.695 m (31 ft 9 11/16 in)
Height, tail up: 3.945 m (12 ft 11 5/16 in)
Wing area: 20.05 m² (215.8 sq ft)
Weights
Empty: 2,490 kg (5,490 lb)
Gross: 3,440 kg (7,580 lb)
Performance
Max speed: 611 km/h (380 mph)
at 6,000 m (19,690 ft)
Time to climb to 6,000 m (19,690 ft):
5 min 50 sec
Service ceiling: 11,520 m (37,800 ft)
Range with one auxiliary drop fuel tank:
1,900 km (1,180 mls)
Armament
2 × 20 mm Type 99 Model 2 Mk 4 cannon
with 210 rpg
2 × 20 mm Type 99 Model 1 Mk 4 cannon
with 190 rpg

Nakajima *Saiun* modified-Mk 11 Night Fighter
(mod. C6N1, Allied Code name: Myrt)

flown by Lieutenant (jg) Hiroshi Yasuda and navigated by Lieutenant (jg) Taro Fukuda, belongs to the 3rd *Hikotai*, 302nd *Kokutai* at Atsugi air base in Kanagawa Prefecture, southwest of Tokyo in July 1945. Converted from carrier-based reconnaissance aircraft *Saiun* Mk 11 (C6N1), and attacked on B-29s in the night of August 1, 1945.

Power unit
Nakajima *Homare* Mk 21 18-cylinder air-cooled engine:
1,990 hp for take-off
1,625 hp at 6,100 m (20,010 ft)

Dimensions
Span: 12.50 m (41 ft 1/8 in)
Length, tail up: 11.12 m (36 ft 5 13/16 in)
Height, tail up: 3.92 m (12 ft 10 5/16 in)
Wing area: 25.5 m² (274.5 sq ft)
Weights
Empty: approx. 2,950 kg (6,500 lb)
Gross: approx. 4,550 kg (10,030 lb)
Performance
Max speed: approx. 580 km/h (360 mph) at 6,000 m (19,690 ft)
Armament
1 × 30 mm Type 5 Mk 1 cannon

Kawasaki Type 3 Mk 1D Fighter *Hien*
(Ki61-ID, Allied Code name: Tony)

flown by Captain Teruhiko Kobayashi, Commander
of the 244th *Hiko-Sentai*, at Chofu airfield in Tokyo,
mid-April 1945. He shot down more than 10 B-29s
including one by ramming attack and two F6Fs.

Power unit
  Kawasaki *Ha* 40 12-cylinder liquid-cooled engine:
  1,175 hp for take-off
  1,100 hp at 4,200 m (13,780 ft)

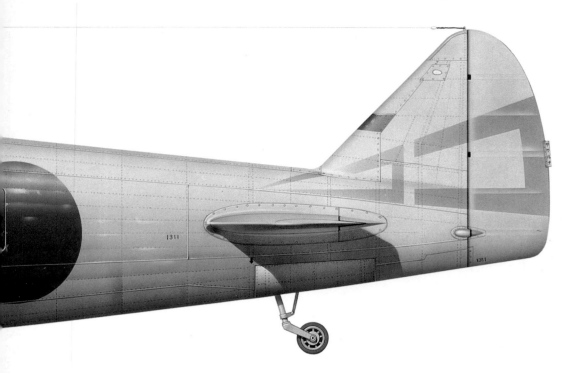

Nakajima Type 2 Mk 2C Fighter *Shoki* (Ki44-IIC, Allied Code name: Tojo)

flown by Captain Yoshio Yoshida, Captain of the 3rd *Chutai*, 70th *Hiko* (Flying)-*Sentai*, at Kashiwa airfield in Chiba Prefecture, northeast of Tokyo, end of May 1945. He shot down six B-29s over Kanto districts from March 10 to May 25, 1945, and scored one unconfirmed victory against B-29 in the daytime over Anshan in Manchuria on September 8, 1944.

Power units
  Nakajima Ha 109 14-cylinder air-cooled engines:
  1,520 hp for take-off
  1,320 hp at 5,250 m (17,225 ft)
Dimensions
  Span: 9.45 m (31 ft)
  Length, tail up: 8.90 m (29 ft 2³/₈ in)
  Height, tail up: 3.248 m (10 ft 7⁷/₈ in)
  Wing area: 15.0 m² (161.5 sq ft)
Weight
  Empty: 2,106 kg (4,643 lb)
  Gross: 2,764 kg (6,093 lb)
Performance
  Max speed: 605 km/h (376 mph) at 5,200 m (17,060 ft)
  Time to climb to 8,000 m (26,250 ft): 9 min 37 sec
  Service ceiling: 11,200 m (36,750 ft)
  Range with two auxiliary drop fuel tanks: 1,600 km (990 mls)
Armament
  4 × 12.7 mm Ho 103 machine guns with 760 rounds in all

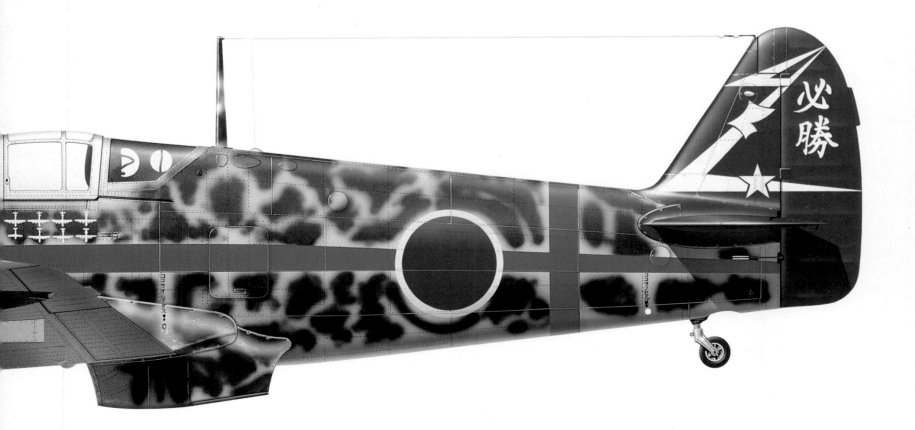

Dimensions
  Span: 12.00 m (39 ft 4⁷/₁₆ in)
  Length, tail up: 8.94 m (29 ft 4 in)
  Height, tail up: 3.40 m (11 ft 1⁷/₈ in)
  Wing area: 20.0 m² (215.3 sq ft)
Weights
  Empty: 2,630 kg (5,800 lb)
  Gross: 3,470 kg (7,650 lb)

Performance
  Max speed: 580 km/h (360 mph) at 5,000 m (16,400 ft)
  Time to climb to 5,000 m (16,400 ft): 7 min
  Service ceiling: 10,000 m (32,810 ft)
  Range without auxiliary drop fuel tanks: 1,800 km (1,120 mls)
Armament
  2 × 20 mm Ho 5 cannon with 120 rounds rpg
  2 × 12.7 mm Ho 103 with 250 rounds rpg

Scale ¹/₂₄

Mitsubishi A6M2 Zeros Fighters belonged to the 3rd *Kokutai* undergo maintenance at Kupang, Timor in 1942. (Yoji Watanabe)

attempted very often.

When the B-17E models arrived, the rules changed, although it took the Japanese fighters a while to realize it. They continued their tail attacks, and the new tail turret, with its power-operated twin .50-cal (12.7 mm) machine guns, picked them off. In one old-fashioned tail assault, the B-17E gunners claimed 11 of 15 interceptors. Again, this figure must be regarded with considerable skepticism. Japanese sources deny that the Tainan and 3rd *Kokutai*s—then fighting the B-17s—ever suffered such a crippling loss.

So they changed their tactics, going around to the front of the bomber and diving on the leader, hoping to break up the formation. Remember that the tight combat box had yet to evolve in the skies over Europe and that the bombers' Vee formation was believed to provide good overlapping fields of fire for defending gunners.

In a typical attack, a few—sometimes only one—of the Japanese attacked from the front. That pilot may have been the most experienced, or the flight leader, because frontal attacks, with their high closing speeds, were dangerous and required great skill and fast reflexes. The rest of the aircraft—always identified as A6M Zeros at this stage of the war, although they were undoubtedly a mix of Zero and Ki43 fighters—flew parallel to the bombers and off to the sides out of range. They peeled off, one at a time, and slashed in on front quarter attacks. During the first six or so months of the war, they seldom made coordinated attacks or approached from more than one heading simultaneously. As a result, when the lone fighter roared in, every gunner that sighted him opened fire and, quite often, shot him down. With two dozen large-caliber machine guns concentrated on a single target, the bombers frequently won those battles.

Two Japanese pilots, more aggressive than the rest, gained temporary fame during these solitary attacks. They dove out of the high frontal position, fired, half-rolled, and dove again through the formation. Gunners had a difficult time trying to follow the fast-moving fighters. Over New Guinea, the gunners encountered, and named, "Wewak Charlie." Above Timor, they were harrassed by "Whirling Willie from Dili." Both were recognized by their steep jinking and aggressive diving attacks. A fighter pilot operating over the Timor sea was "Honest John from Ambon," known for his straight-in diving attacks that were carried to point-blank range.

After mid-1942, USAAF bomber squadrons reported fewer and lighter Japanese intercepting forces and that Japanese pilots seemed somewhat inferior in quality to those

encountered earlier. But also by this time, Japanese experiments to find optimum attack angles against B-17s and B-24s were paying off. They settled on the frontal assault as best, approaching from head-on or slightly below the bombers. They also developed coordinated attacks, using parallel streams of fighters on each side of the bomber formation, attacking in rotation from opposite sides. Japanese pilots were reported coming in closer during their firing runs and holding their fire longer than customary.

B-17 and B-24 formations reported variations on the basic interception schemes. In one post-combat report, crews said that the fighters made their main attack from head-on positions, while secondary attacks were made from below and abeam in the apparent hopes of scoring while gunners were concentrating on the main attack. In other engagements, the fighters lined up in trail on each side of the bomber formation and came in, again individually, on the nose quarters, then diving underneath or breaking out into a chandelle for another attack.

In the Aleutians, where Japanese fighters were float-plane models of the Zero, the B-17s bombed from altitudes as high as 30,000 ft (9,100 m). At that height, performance of the Japanese fighters suffered; they were not much of a threat. Against B-24 bombers, the Japanese did somewhat better by coordinating attacks. But most of the time the fighters remained distant and seemed satisfied with harassment of the bombers during their bomb run.

Bomber crews in the Aleutians first reported an odd propensity of Japanese fighters. Out of gun range, they performed aerobatics—slow and fast rolls, spiral climbs and dives, Immelman turns, chandelles—apparently with the intent of distracting bomber crews before attacking or while others attacked from opposite quarter.

The story was basically the same in the China-Burma-India theater of war. Bomber crews first reported Ki61 fighters here and believed them to be Japanese versions of the Bf109. (In the heat of combat, there was a resemblance. But regardless of resemblance, Japanese sources claim that Ki61s did not fight in the CBI theater.) Here also the bomber crews first were attacked by Japanese Ki45-*Kai* twin-engined fighters in combat above Rangoon. The attacks came from two o'clock and ten o'clock high, and the fighters recovered under the bombers. The Japanese feinted effectively, drawing bomber turrets in one direction to cover the real attack from the opposite direction.

A lone B-17 flew a reconnaissance mission over the Solomon Islands on a fine May day in 1942. Seven Zeros—a for-

Starting of the 21st *Hiko-Sentai*'s Ki45-*Kai* A *Toryu*. Fighters of the *Hiko-Sentai* intercepted B-24s over Rangoon in 1943. (Yoji Watanabe)

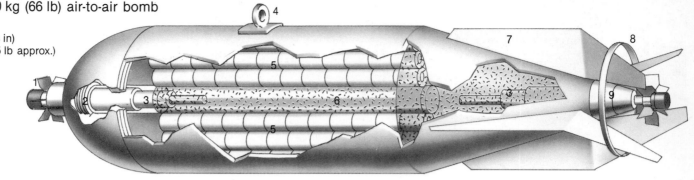

Type 99 No.3 Model 3 30 kg (66 lb) air-to-air bomb

Length: 693 mm (2 ft 3⁵/₁₆ in)
Body diameter: 147 mm (5¹³/₁₆ in)
Total weight: 34 kg approx. (75 lb approx.)

1 Vanes
2 Igniter
3 Fuzes
4 Suspension lug
5 Bomblets
6 Exploder
7 Tail fins
8 Ring strut
9 Clockwork time igniter

mation of four, and a trio—intercepted the Fortress. The four climbed above and out of range of the bomber's guns, and the other three took position on the port side, out of range and flying parallel to the bomber. The four overhead then dropped "…small objects which exploded on a level with, but some 75—150 feet (23—46 m) astern of, the B-17." After the bombs burst, the trio of Zeros attacked from beam positions, closing to 150 yards (140 m) while firing. The other four again climbed to position above the B-17 and repeated the bombing. The bomber crew got home to tell the story, reporting that the bombs produced a "…waterfall effect of streamers with red fire at the end of every streamer."

Air-to-air bombing attempts were tried during WWII by the British and the Germans as well as the Japanese. Properly placed, a substantial bomb burst in the middle of a formation can do more damage than anti-aircraft fire. A much heavier explosive charge can be carried to altitude by a fighter than by an anti-aircraft shell. That was the route taken by the Germans; the Japanese seem to have opted for a shotgun effect. The bombs developed for their air-to-air bombing assaults contained clusters of bomblets, ranging in weight from a fraction of a kilogram to one kilogram (2.2 lb).

The usual Japanese tactic was to drop from above the formation, using time-delay fuses set for eight to ten seconds. The drop altitude was an estimated 1,000 m (3,300 ft) above the bombers, and the bombing was followed by conventional attacks. For more than a year, these bombings produced little result. But the Japanese persisted, trying out combinations of tactics and weapons, developing short-delay fuses for phosphorus and high-explosive bombs. Special wing racks gave fighters the capability of carrying ten 30 kg (66 lb) bombs and, by late 1944, these attacks had become effective and deadly. They were, said intelligence reports, standard procedures against both B-24 and B-29 formations, and they were "…a serious nuisance and potential threat."

Bombing involved four basic attacks: high-level, low-level, dive-bombing, and a combination of dive bombing and gunnery run. The high-level assault was typified by the run on the lone B-17 above the Solomons. The low-level attack was totally different. Generally a formation of four fighters approached in line abreast from the bomber's 12 o'clock position and about 100 m (330 ft) above the formation. At a distance of about 1,000 m (3,300 ft), all four fighters salvoed their bombs.

According to USAAF intelligence reports, the four-plane bombing formation was part of an organized attack unit that used 16 planes: four bomb-carrying fighters and 12 fighter escorts. If the bombers were escorted, four "bombers" and four fighters attacked the heavies; the remaining eight tackled the bomber escorts. After the bomb drop, it was the usual

air combat free-for-all.

Dive bombing was another variation. Alone or paired, the fighters came in on a 20-degree angle dive from points about 1,000 m (3,300 ft) above and well ahead of the formation. They leveled off about 100 m (330 ft) above and released the bombs about 1,000 m (3,300 ft) in front. When the bombs burst, the fighters broke into chandelles left and right, then attacked in the conventional way.

By late 1944, Japanese fighters had developed a very effective coordinated attack against B-24 formations. Five or more fighters in a closed-up trail formation bored in at 12 o'clock high. The first two bombed the formation, then broke in dives to the left and right. The remaining three had begun a dive when the bombs were released, timed to arrive in firing position just after the bombs went off. They attacked from head-on, at high speed and firing continuously. The favorite time for this, and all the air-to-air bombing tactics, was during the final run-in to the target, when the heavy bombers were flying straight and level.

Bombs used for this purpose included the Army's *Ta-Dan* bomb, developed for air-to-ground use against airfields. This came in two versions: one of 50 kg (110 lb) with 76 bomblets weighing 0.4 kg (0.9 lb), and the other of 30 kg (66 lb) with 30 of the 0.4 kg bomblets. The Navy had developed a bomb, specifically for air-to-air attacks, which also came in two sizes: The 30 kg (66 lb) Type 99 No. 3 Model 3 with 144 bomblets weighing 0.2 kg (0.44 lb), and the 250 kg (551 lb) Type 2 No. 25 Model 3 with either 780 or 1,086 of the 0.2 kg bomblets.

Two 50 kg (110 lb) *Ta-Dan*s beneath the fuselage of Ki46-IIIB reconnaissance aircraft from the 17th Independent Squadron. (Shunsaku Myodo)

The 7th AF B-24s under the attack of 30 kg (66 lb) Model 3 air-to-air bombs dropped by Zero Fighters over Iwo Jima in 1944. (USAF)

The American raids on Lae and Rabaul, two major Japanese fighter bases in the South Pacific, inspired the development of a new arrangement of aircraft armament. The Tainan *Kokutai*, a crack fighter unit deployed to those bases, included an inventive officer, Cdr. Yasuna Kozono, who proposed converting a Navy land-based reconnaissance aircraft—the twin-engined Nakajima J1N1-C—into a night fighter. The Zero fighters operated by the Tainan unit were no good for night work. The J1N1-C, originally designed as a long-range fighter, had been adopted as a reconnaissance aircraft. Kozono started thinking of the conventional air-to-air bombing attack but soon considered using cannon firing downward to do the same job more effectively. Firing upward should produce equal results, he reasoned.

Four obliquely mounted 20 mm Type 99 cannon set in the fuselage of a Nakajima J1N1 night Fighter *Gekko*. (National Archives)

Kozono had, in fact, also devised what the Germans called "*Schräge Musik*," and at essentially the same time in mid-1943. Was this a case of parallel invention or of an exchange of information? It may never be known; but the fact is that the Japanese were first in the field and first in combat.

It was a radical idea, and Kozono began to fight the bureaucracy to get action. Eventually he succeeded, and two J1N1s were converted to the new configuration. The Tainan unit (later redesignated the 251st *Kokutai* after a few months back in Japan) returned to action at Rabaul in May 1943 but with only one of the converted fighters. The other had been wiped out in a crash landing. Remember that they had guns, but not radar, and the Japanese night fighter pilots were required to use "cat's eyes" techniques to find bombers by night.

On the night of May 21, 1943, Chief Petty Officer Shigetoshi Kudo maneuvered his J1N1 into position under a B-17E beginning a bomb run on Vunakanau Airfield near Rabaul, New Britain. Kudo sighted, opened fire, and blasted the bomber. He repeated his performance with a second B-17E. (The first German "*Schräge Musik*" victory occurred three months later.)

The new fighters were given the name of *Gekko* (Moonlight), and the Navy command approved additional conversions. The unit, although being equipped with more and more *Gekko* night fighters, never managed to keep more than two on a combat-ready status. Maintenance and logistics helped defeat the first Japanese night fighter.

The 251st was finally recognized officially as Japan's first night fighter unit. Zero day fighters and their pilots were transferred, and the 251st unit strength was established at 24 night fighters. That was optimistic; actual strength seldom exceeded nine, with four or five ready to fight.

Events in the South Pacific overtook the *Gekko* night fighters. Their base on Rabaul was bypassed by the Allied forces and beyond resupply capability by the Japanese. During April 1944, the two that were left on Rabaul flew to Truk and, as far as is known, ended the war there. But we will meet *Gekko* again in the skies over Japan.

Fighting the Firestorms

A dozen Nakajima Ki43 *Hayabusa* (Oscar) fighters cruised at 14,000 ft (4,300 m) over the rugged terrain that divided India and Burma. April 26, 1944, was clear and visibility was excellent, an asset in flight over the menacing mountains. One Japanese pilot spotted a glint in the sky about five miles (8 km) away and a couple of thousand feet (600 m) above. Six fighters broke formation and climbed to the intercept.

In the single B-29, Major Charles Hanson saw the six fighters, watched them split into threes and take positions on each side of his B-29, out of gunnery range. Hanson was edgy; his B-29 carried an extra 2,000 gallons (7,570 ltr) of aviation fuel to deliver from India to a forward base at Chengtu, China.

The Ki43s paced the B-29 for about 15 miles (24 km), establishing speed, looking at its defenses, judging angles for attack. Then the lead Ki43 decided it was time, swung in behind and below the B-29, and opened fire at about 400 yards (360 m). The B-29 tail cannon jammed, and its machine guns wouldn't fire; worse, three of four machine guns in the top turret also jammed. While tail gunner Sergeant Harold Lanham tried to get his guns working again, Hanson pulled the bomber into a climb. Two more fighters swung in, fired, and missed. Lanham got his guns working again; as a Ki43 bored in close, Lanham fired and hit, later claiming a probable.

The other *Hayabusa* fighters made several more firing passes at the B-29, then inexplicably broke off the intercept and headed away. It was the first encounter between Japanese interceptors and the new American heavy bomber, an engagement that would become a battle the B-29s would win finally and decisively. This chapter describes the valiant but fruitless efforts made by Japanese interceptors to stop the B-29s.

Although a policy had been established in 1922 assigning home defense to the Army, assisted by the Navy, all indications are that the Japanese armed forces did not take seriously the possibility of a future need for air defenses. But by May 1944, the Japanese Command finally had accepted the belief that the Allies would try to invade Japan. However, the Command also believed that combined air and naval attacks by the Japanese Army and Navy would defeat the attempt. That view changed as Japanese outposts continued to collapse under combined air and naval pressure from the Allies; staff

Angles of defensive fire in Boeing B-29 Superfortress

B-29-5-MO of the 498th BG, 73rd BW, U.S. 20th AF, based at Isley (Isely) Field, Saipan in the Mariana Islands in early 1945.

1 General Electric upper forward turret: 4 (early type: 2) × 0.5 in (12.7 mm) Browning M2 machine guns
2 General Electric lower forward turret: 2 × 0.50 in M2 guns
3 General Electric upper rear turret: 2 × 0.50 in M2 guns
4 General Electric lower rear turret: 2 × 0.50 in M2 guns
5 Boeing designed tail turret: 1 × 20 mm M2B cannon (deleted with later models) and 2 × 0.50 in M2 guns

officers then glimpsed a grim future, a heavy air onslaught led by USAAF bombers.

The Japanese Army General Defense Command, assigned to repel invaders as well as fight off hostile aircraft, included three subordinate commands: Eastern, Central, and Western. Each had an air division, an anti-aircraft artillery group, and an air raid warning unit. In an obvious anomaly, anti-aircraft defense of the increasing number of military air bases was left to the local commanders at each airfield, separate from the GDC units.

Mitsubishi *Raiden* Mk 21 (J2M3) interceptors from the 302nd *Kokutai*'s Atsugi air base on the patrol flight around Mt. Fuji in August 1944. (Yoji Watanabe)

Power units: 4 × 2,200 hp Wright R-3350-23 engines
Span: 141 ft 3 in (43.05 m)
Length, level position: 99 ft 0 in (30.17 m)
Height, on the ground: 27 ft 9 in (8.46 m)
Wing area: 1,736 sq ft (161.3 m²)
Gross weight: 134,000 lb (60,780 kg)
Max speed: 357 mph (575 km/h) at 25,000 ft (7,620 m)
Range with 20,000 lb (9,070 kg) bombs: 3,150 mls (5,070 km)
Service ceiling: 31,850 ft (9,710 m)
Bomb load: 20,000 lb (9,070 kg)
Crew: 11

Eastern Command was responsible for the political and industrial heart of Japan, the Kanto plain, which held Tokyo, Yokohama, and Kawasaki and was a center of rice production. It was accepted as the most vital portion of Japan and would be defended to the end by citizens with spears and clubs if necessary.

Central Command guarded the area around Osaka, Kobe, and Nagoya; the Western Command was responsible for Kyushu, the western area of Honshu island, and southwest Shikoku. In this region was the mammoth Imperial Iron & Steel Works at Yahata (Yawata).

The air units attached to these commands were notably weak. Their fighters were predominantly old standbys: the Ki43, Ki44 *Shoki* (Tojo), and the Ki84 *Hayate* (Frank), all

manufactured by Nakajima, and the Ki45-*Kai Toryu* (Nick), Ki61 *Hien* (Tony), and Ki100, all manufactured by Kawasaki.

The Ki43 was obsolescent, totally outclassed in performance by the B-29; the Ki44 was the only fighter officially classed as an interceptor by the Japanese Army and was also deficient in performance. The Ki84 was a superlative fighter, probably the best fielded by the Japanese; but very few were available for the homeland defense when the B-29s first came over.

The Japanese relied heavily on the Ki45-*Kai* for night interceptions. It was intended to carry airborne radar but seldom, if ever, was so equipped. The Ki61 lacked altitude performance and was rarely seen at B-29 altitudes. The Ki100 was an outstanding fighter, basically a radial-engined Ki61, but

Two veteran naval Pilots of the 332nd *Kokutai* show their fighting against B-29 at Naruo air base between Osaka and Kobe. (Yoji Watanabe)

Remains of a B-29 belonged to the 462nd BG, 58th BW, in the 21st Naval Air Arsenal's hangar. This bomber was shot down by the 352nd *Kokutai* on November. 21. 1944. (Hiroshi Minematsu)

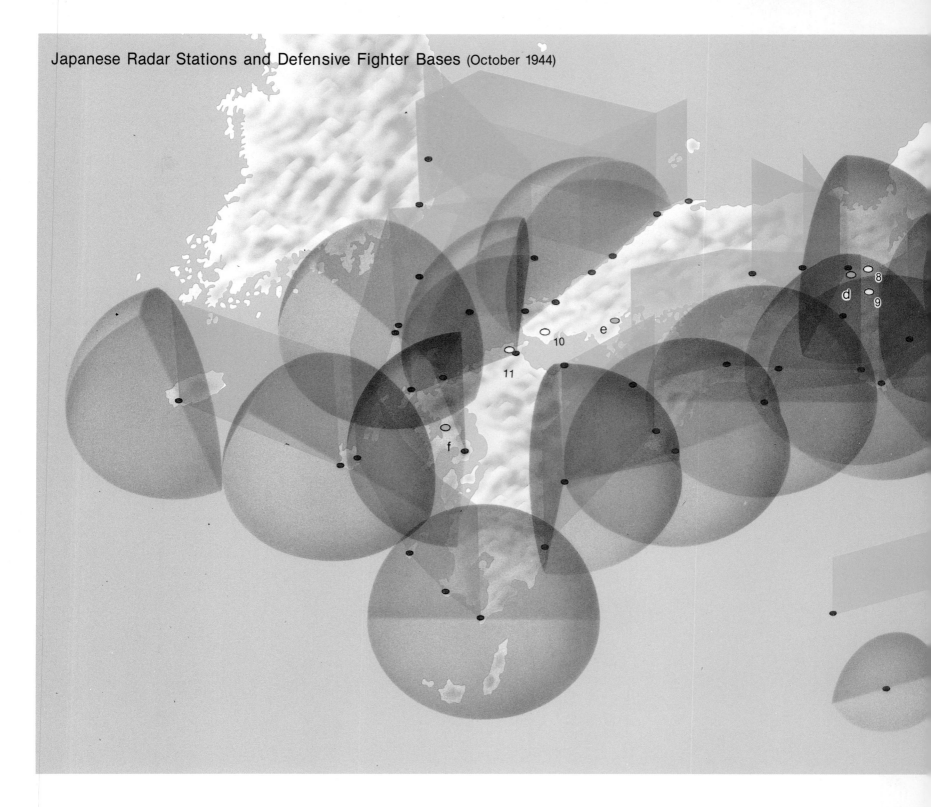

few ever became operational. The first prototype Ki100 was completed late in January 1945. Probably less than half of all these aircraft were capable of night flying, and few of the pilots had any night-flying experience anyway.

The equipment of the 12th Air Division in the Western sector was typical: 35 Ki45-*Kai* twin-engined fighters, 10 of which were equipped for night flying, and 25 Ki61 single-engined fighters, with four capable of night operations. The pilots assigned to the Ki61 were raw, unfamiliar with the airplane, and few had acceptable night-flying experience. This ineffective organization defended Japan's main steel plant.

Other aircraft were available for home defense but not to the Army. Only the Navy could command and control its own fighter fleets, which included the Kawanishi N1K1-J *Shiden* (George), with poor altitude performance; the Mitsubishi A6M *Reisen* (Zeke) series, and the J2M *Raiden* (Jack), the latter an excellent interceptor. Later, three Navy types were used as night fighters after modifications: Nakajima's J1N2/J1N3 *Gekko* (Irving), and the P1Y1-S *Ginga* (Francis) and D4Y2-S *Suisei*

(Judy), both built by *Kaigun Koku-Gijutsusho* (the Naval Aero-Technical Arsenal).

The air defenses included anti-aircraft artillery, searchlights, radar, some barrage balloon installations, picket-boats offshore, and observer posts. Each was at a technical or operational level far below either the British or German equivalents.

The Japanese Navy's first early warning radar Model 1 Mk 1 was emplaced at Katsuura in Chiba Prefecture during November 1941. It had a useful range of about 250 km (155 mls) against a large formation of aircraft, and of about 130 km (80 mls) against a single aircraft. In December 1941, the Army had a single type of Doppler radar—Type A— in operation. Type A radars had very simple efficiency and could only detect something that flew through the beams. In the summer of 1942, these were supplemented by Type B units that had a useful range out to about 200–250 km (125–155 mls). They could not judge the altitude of a target and could not differentiate the radar signature of a B-29 from that of a P-51. It was late in 1944

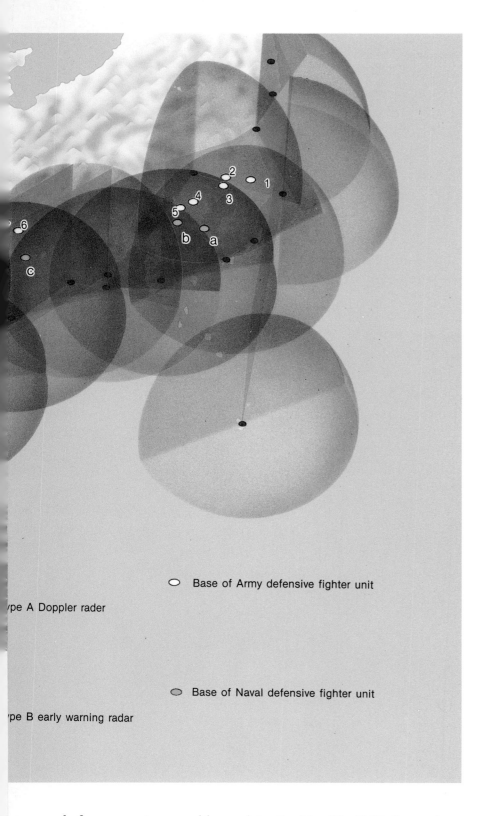

Army fighter units

The 10th *Hiko-Shidan* (Air Division)
1. The 23rd *Hiko-Sentai* (Ki43 and Ki44), Base: Inba
2. The 18th *Hiko-Sentai* (Ki61), Base: Kashiwa
3. The 53rd *Hiko-Sentai* (Ki45-*Kai*), Base: Matsudo
4. The 47th *Hiko-Sentai* (Ki44), Base: Narimasu
5. The 244th *Hiko-Sentai* (Ki61), Base: Chofu
   The 11th *Hiko-Shidan*
6. The 55th *Hiko-Sentai* (Ki61), Base: Komaki
7. The 5th *Hiko-Sentai* (Ki45-Kai), Base: Kiyosu
8. The 56th *Hiko-Sentai* (Ki61), Base: Itami
   (The night fighter unit of the 332nd *Kokutai* stayed in the same base
   from December 1944)
9. The 246th *Hiko-Sentai* (Ki44), Base: Taisho
   The 12th *Hiko-Shidan*
10. The 4th *Hiko-Sentai* (Ki45-*kai*), Base: Ozuki
11. The 59th *Hiko-Sentai* (Ki61), Base: Ashiya

Main defense areas

The 18th, 23rd, 47th, 53rd and 244th *Hiko-Sentai*s:
  Tokyo-Yokohama-Kawasaki area
The 5th and 55th *Hiko-Sentai*s: Nagoya area
The 56th and 246th *Hiko-Sentai*s: Osaka-Kobe area
The 4th and 59th *Hiko-Sentai*s: Kokura-Yahata (Yawata)-Fukuoka area

Naval fighter units
a. The Yokosuka *Kokutai* (A6M, J2M, N1K1-J, J1N, D4Y2-S), Base: Yokosuka
b. The 302nd *Kokutai* (A6M, J2M, J1N, P1Y1-S, D4Y2-S), Base: Atsugi
c. The 210th *Kokutai* (A6M, N1K1-J, J1N), Base: Meiji
d. The day fighter unit of the 332nd *Kokutai* (A6M, J2M),
   Base: Naruo (from December 1944)
e. The 332nd *Kokutai* (A6M, J2M, J1N, D4Y2-S), Base: Iwakuni (until December 1944)
f. The 352nd *Kokutai* (A6M, J2M, J1N, D4Y2-S), Base: Omura

Main defense areas
The Yokosuka and 302nd *Kokutai*s: Yokosuka-Yokohama-Tokyo area
The 210th *Kokutai*: Nagoya area
The 332nd *Kokutai*: Kure-Iwakuni and Osaka-Kobe areas
The 352nd *Kokutai*: Sasebo-Nagasaki area

○ Base of Army defensive fighter unit

pe A Doppler rader

◐ Base of Naval defensive fighter unit

pe B early warning radar

before operators could consistently identify B-29 formations and estimate altitude and speed of flight.

The picketboats, one of which had flashed the early warning of the Doolittle raid, were not of much help after that raid. They had radios, but not radar. When the Eastern Army Command was ordered to form a new unit, it equipped one boat with radar and another without and stationed them 200 miles (320 km) offshore. The radar almost immediately needed repair, and the picketboat put back to a shore base for the work. It was sunk in March 1945 after a short and almost useless career.

In August 1943, Eastern Command had 350 AA guns, of both 75 mm and 80 mm caliber; by November 1, 1944, when the first F-13 reconnaissance flight appeared over the Kanto plain, that force had strengthened considerably. It numbered 316 75 mm guns, 186 80 mm guns, and 26 120 mm heavy guns with 61 Mark I, II, III, and IV radar directors. These weapons were deployed primarily around Tokyo, Yokohama, and Kawasaki. The Navy centralized most of its anti-aircraft artillery near

Yokosuka. Within a couple of weeks after the first F-13 appearance, Eastern Command received another 23 80 mm and 12 75 mm guns, with two Mark III radar directors.

Japanese radars operated at even lower frequencies than the German radars, and so "window," or "chaff" as it was generally called by USAAF crews, was nearly useless. The equivalent job was done by long strips of aluminum foil, one inch (2.5 cm) wide by several hundred feet long, and universally called "rope" by the B-29 crews that dumped out millions of feet of the stuff over Japan. Many of the Japanese AA gun units used Mark III radar directors based on, or copied from, British gun-laying radars captured at Singapore. Knowing that, it was easy to devise a specific jammer unit.

Radio monitoring of USAAF transmissions was one of the best early-warning aids the Japanese had. American pilots continually used the radios, hardly ever observed radio silence, and the Japanese often gained first knowledge of an incoming raid and its intended targets because of slipshod American radio security.

The Japanese saw the B-29 as the primary, perhaps the only, antagonist and began to devise or adapt special methods to attack the heavy bombers. Training units, with a limited number of fighters assigned, manned these aircraft with instructors and test pilots to augment regular Army air units. But that concept did not prove out. Between a lack of unit training and the requirements of other duties, the results were so poor that the augmenting units were disbanded after less than a year.

The shortage of oil—all of it imported and little of it stored—posed perhaps the greatest problem. Pilot training had suffered; pilots were coming to combat units with less than 100 hours of flying time, a far cry from the experience levels of the pilots that had manned fighter units at the beginning of the war. But to train longer and harder would take precious fuel needed for fighting.

The 10th AD had dispatched units in strength to try to intercept several lone F-13 reconnaissance flights made over their sector during November 1944. They failed miserably, never getting near the enemy. Flight tests made by the Division proved that only its very best pilots could nurse their fighters up to B-29 operating altitudes above 30,000 ft (9,100 m). The highest any of them ever had gone was 36,000 ft (11,000 m). It would be impossible for the entire air division to reach those altitudes, even if the airplanes they were flying had been trouble-free.

So Japan's air defenses depended on fighters with inadequate altitude performance and pilots with insufficient experience, hampered by a lack of tactical training and a shortage of fuel. Radars couldn't discriminate among targets; searchlights couldn't be pointed with any degree of accuracy, and only the heaviest anti-aircraft artillery could loft its shells to the operating heights of the big bombers.

Desperate circumstances sometimes suggest desperate actions. In late 1944, the idea of ramming attacks—*Taiatari* (body-crashing) in Japanese—was broached as a possible means of defending against the B-29s. One fighter and its pilot was an advantageous trade for a B-29 and its 11 men. The concept had been tried with some success as early as 1943, probably more in frustration than as a matter of tactical policy.

On November 7, 1944, Maj. Gen. Kihachiro Yoshida, commander of the 10th Air Division, ordered the formation of special attack units—the euphemism for suicide flights—in each fighter *Sentai*. The established force was four Ki44s each from the 23rd, 47th, and 70th *Sentai*s, four Ki45-*Kai*s from the 53rd, and four Ki61s from the 244th.

Following the first Tokyo raid by B-29 formations on November 24, 1944, the special attack units were doubled in strength, and the 12th AD formed two units of eight aircraft each of Ki45-*Kai* and Ki61. The 10th AD units were designated *Shinten* (Shaking Heaven)-*Tai*, and those of the 12th were named *Kaiten* (Reversing Heaven)-*Tai*.

Altitude performance was gained by completely stripping these aircraft of armor and armament, losing between 150 and 200 kg (330 and 440 lb) of dead weight in the process. The Ki45-*Kai*s were modified to single-seat configuration by covering the rear position with sheet metal.

Even so, the fighters had great difficulty getting an

The Kawasaki Ki61-ID *Hien* flown by Captain Teruhiko Kobayashi, Commander of the 244th *Hiko-Sentai*. Note the sixth victory mark by the ramming attack on January. 27, 1945. (Chieko Kobayashi)

altitude advantage on the bombers, so that the suggested attack style was modified to a shallow dive from the front. But such an approach required considerable pilot skill, and the inexperienced pilots in the special units just did not have those skills. They received an absolute minimum of training, a mistake made also in Germany. In spite of the built-in failure mode, these suicidal attacks were continued until the very end of the war in the air, although most special attack units had been disbanded by late spring of 1945.

Air-to-air bombing had been useful, if not very effective, against B-17 and B-24 formations; Japanese tacticians extended the attack to formations of the B-29s. The first reports of the use of those *Ta-Dan* or Model 3 bomb tactics against B-29s came after the raid on Okayama, Formosa, October 14, 1944. Nine fighters dropped phosphorus bombs on the formation, with inconclusive results.

Again the superior altitude performance of the big bombers was the key defense. The bomb-carrying fighters could not climb above Superfortress operating altitudes. The 5th *Hiko-Sentai* in the 11th Air Division stripped its Ki45-*Kai* night fighters of everything but armament and radios. They were able to gain some 20–30 km/h (12–19 mph) speed and a few hundred feet altitude, and kept trying the *Ta-Dan* air-to-air

Four Nakajima Ki44-IIB *Shoki* fighters of *Shinten-Tai*, belonged to the 47th *Hiko-Sentai*, going to take off from Narimasu airfield, Tokyo in the winter of 1944–45 (Yoji Watanabe)

B-29s from 9th BG, 313rd BW, head for their target. The upper forward turret gunner prepares for firing against vertical descent attack by Japanese fighters. (Yoji Watanabe)

bombing techniques, along with other interception tactics.

Later, when the B-29s bombed from lower altitudes, the *Ta-Dan* tactic was tried repeatedly. On the April 7, 1945, strike against the infamous Target 357—the Nakajima engine factory at Musashino, Tokyo—the B-29 force came in at 12,000 ft (3,660 m), determined to destroy the factory. Japanese interceptors made 130 reported attacks with phosphorus bombs.

In the defense of Japan, time was a powerful adversary. Consider the time lines of a B-29 raid and the Japanese response. Japanese early warning radar could detect a B-29 raid at a maximum range of less than 300 km (190 mls). Because of Japan's island geography, no radar was much more than 200 km (120 mls) from a B-29 objective. So the bombers could often get within 300 miles (480 km) of their targets before being detected and could be over the target in less than an hour after detection.

At a minimum, and when everything was going well, it took 20 minutes to pass a first warning from the radar sites through the chain of command to a fighter unit, and then it took most of an hour for those fighters to scramble and climb to B-29 operating altitudes. Intercepts, if any, generally took place either through lucky deployment of fighter forces or on the outbound leg after the targets had been hit.

Most Japanese fighters had an endurance of about two hours. To scramble and climb to B-29 altitude took one of those hours, and to let down and land took a half-hour. That left only a half-hour maximum time for any combat operations or for loitering in an area where an interception might take place.

There was another problem; Japanese aircraft performance suffered at high altitude. To attack bombers or to combat their escorts, fighters need maneuverability that is gained generally at high altitude by engine power. But above 8,000 m (26,000 ft), Japanese fighters lacked the required power and in addition had to be handled very carefully, almost gingerly, to avoid stalling out in turns or under g loads. Japanese sources report that it was difficult to maintain control at high altitudes and that the fighters' stability characteristics suffered. "Even a

slight bank resulted in a loss of altitude that might take 10 or 20 minutes to regain."

One Japanese report states: "So successful were the enemy's diversionary tactics, that they often were able to penetrate into key target areas and begin bombing before the plotters and interceptors were able to determine the probable target...(Our) disposition of forces seldom coincided with the true battle situation and when it did, it was generally due to chance or coincidence."

Night interceptions were planned around a system of established intercept zones, with dependence on searchlights to find and illuminate the B-29s. Some rudimentary radio navigation aids existed, but they were installed at home bases and were most effective in bringing fighters home, rather than in aiding their navigation to an intercept. Bad weather and darkness kept most of the Japanese interception force on the ground.

In the winter of 1944, small-scale night raids increased and spurred attempts to train interceptor pilots for night flying. The first-ever Japanese night fighter unit, the 53rd *Hiko-Sentai*, had been formed on March 23, 1944. It immediately established a very strict training regiment. Pilots trained every night and tried to sleep during the day. They wore dark glasses if they had to go out in the daylight.

A Japanese document states that the training was so intensive that "...morale deteriorated within the organization. In addition, a number of nervous breakdowns were suffered by the pilots." It took nearly a year before the 53rd flew its first night combat mission on March 9, 1945. It was a short-lived experiment; the 53rd was taken off its night mission on May 23.

After the B-29 fire raids began on March 9, 1945, Army night fighters were almost useless. They still had no effective radars, and searchlight units were not effective. The only chance interceptors had was to climb above the bomber formations and attack as they were silhouetted against burning cities.

The Navy had completed the development of the *Koku-Gijutsusho* FD-2 AI radar in August 1944 and, by early 1945, had installed some in J1N3 aircraft for service tests. But the tests were unsatisfactory; further, the radars were installed

Nakajima night fighter *Gekko* Mk 11a (J1N3, Irving)

flown by WO Juzo Kuramoto and navigated by Lt (jg) Shiro Kurotori of the Yokosuka *Kokutai*. They shot down five B-29s over Kanto districts, around Tokyo, in the night of August 25–26, 1945. Victory marks of six kills and two damaged are painted on the rear fuselage.

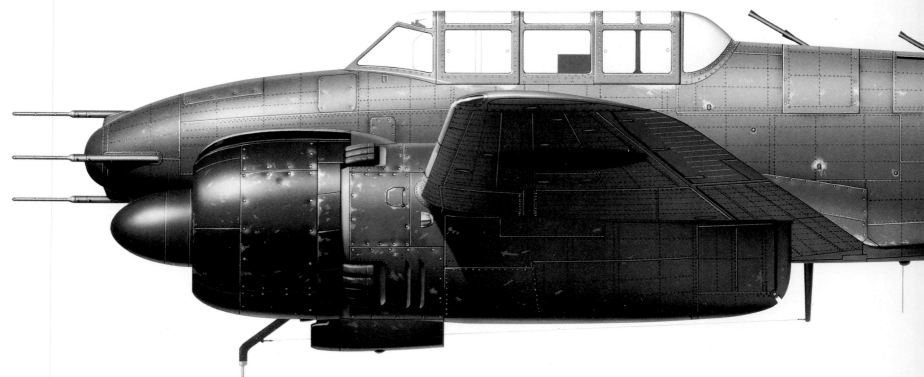

in fighters that were slower than the B-29s, so a rear intercept—the conventional approach in night attacks—was impossible anyway. Although the 302nd, 332nd, and 352nd *Kokutai*s received some J1N3 night fighters equipped with FD-2 radars, many Japanese pilots removed the equipment and gained some performance as a result of a 70 kg (150 lb) weight reduction.

The Japanese at long last translated the handwriting on the wall. On April 15, 1945, about four months before the most devastating air attacks in history, the Air General Army was formed. It was an Army command, in charge of all air units in the home islands. As individual units reported their collected strength for the final battle, the picture became more dismal each day. In late July, 10th Air Division counted 95 serviceable planes: 13 standard Ki43s and seven of an advanced model, 15 Ki44s, 30 Ki45-*Kais*, 15 Ki61s, and 15 Ki84s. The 11th Air Division numbered 130 fighters. The 12th, with only 56 fighters to begin with, made no known report.

Though ordered to intercept every single aircraft that came over the islands after the two atomic bombs had been detonated, the Commander of the 10th Air Division failed to spur his pilots to aggressive attack. It seemed absurd, a Japanese report stated, to incur additional losses with the war obviously lost.

Postwar analyses showed that Japanese fighter opposition was determined, but light, in comparison to German interceptions. Bomber and escort airmen reported more than 11,000 fighter attacks over the home islands, or about one for every three sorties. They were heaviest against the early raids, then tapered off as fuel shortages, pilot losses, and inferior replacement pilots and aircraft became factors in the combat equations. Some of the B-29 raids roared through Japanese skies completely unopposed, except by occasional flak.

Another way to judge the intensity of Japanese opposition was by the claims made by B-29 gunners and by the numbers of bombers that fell victim to fighters. Total B-29 losses in combat from all causes—AA guns, fighters' mid-air collisions—were 494 aircraft. The gunners claimed 714 fighters destroyed, 456 probably destroyed, and 770 damaged. These figures are far below comparable ones for the Battle of Europe and, if they were inflated comparably, only emphasize further the weakness of Japanese air defenses.

It's startling to learn that no more than 26 percent of the total Japanese fighter force was ever assigned to the home defense mission. Beginning in September 1944, between 30 and 40 percent of the Army's air-defense fighters were deployed from the home islands to the Philippines. Most of that force was eventually lost there. In December 1944, by which time the strength of the USAAF bomber force was perfectly obvious, only 17 percent of the fighter force was on the defensive. And at the end of the war, Japan mustered only 16 percent of its effective air force for the last-ditch defense. A total of 535 home defense aircraft faced the thousands the Allied Air Forces and Navy could put over the islands in August 1945.

Industry, often credited for exceptional performance under fire, did in fact turn out large numbers of aircraft. But between a third and a half of them were rejected by the military from the summer of 1944 on, because of the quality of workmanship. Although thousands of aircraft were produced, maintenance and logistics problems reduced the front-line force to only a few hundred. And in actual day-to-day operation, strengths were measured in 10s and 20s.

In studying the Battle of Japan, historians must wonder at the determination of quite ordinary individuals who presumably were intelligent enough to know their fate and yet defied it at the risk of their own lives.

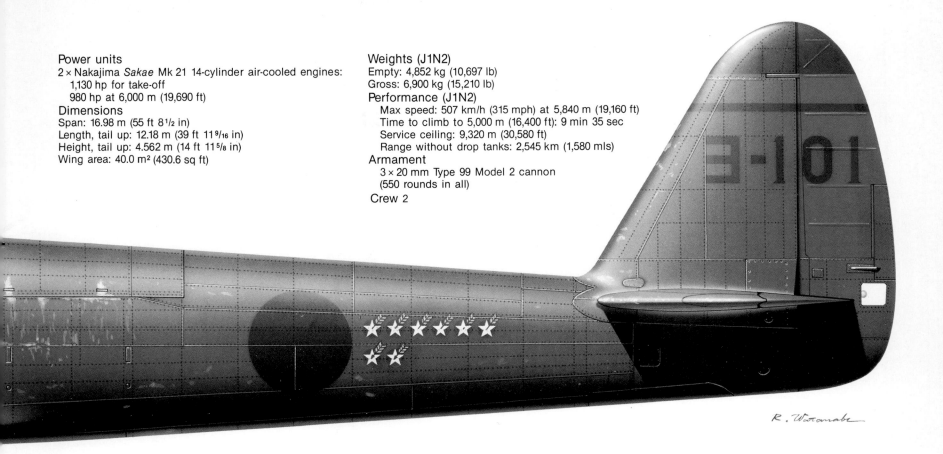

Power units
2 × Nakajima *Sakae* Mk 21 14-cylinder air-cooled engines:
   1,130 hp for take-off
   980 hp at 6,000 m (19,690 ft)
Dimensions
Span: 16.98 m (55 ft 8 1/2 in)
Length, tail up: 12.18 m (39 ft 11 9/16 in)
Height, tail up: 4.562 m (14 ft 11 5/8 in)
Wing area: 40.0 m² (430.6 sq ft)

Weights (J1N2)
Empty: 4,852 kg (10,697 lb)
Gross: 6,900 kg (15,210 lb)
Performance (J1N2)
   Max speed: 507 km/h (315 mph) at 5,840 m (19,160 ft)
   Time to climb to 5,000 m (16,400 ft): 9 min 35 sec
   Service ceiling: 9,320 m (30,580 ft)
   Range without drop tanks: 2,545 km (1,580 mls)
Armament
   3 × 20 mm Type 99 Model 2 cannon
   (550 rounds in all)
Crew 2

R. Watanabe

Weapons of Desperation

Even as World War II wound down to its last weeks of combat, scientists and engineers in Germany and Japan continued to search for just one more weapon to hold off the advancing enemy long enough to make a difference. Surely they could buy time, probably earn easier treatment after surrender, possibly even turn the tide.

And so the final months of the war saw a plethora of proposals and prototypes for radical, even revolutionary, new aircraft and missiles, each hoped to be that one weapon that would save the day. The fascination of what might have been leads to the final chapter of this study of interceptors against heavy bombers.

In May 1944, the Technical Department of the German Air Ministry (*Technischen Amt, Reichsluftfahrt Ministerium*) asked German aircraft companies to propose designs for a target-defense interceptor combining the characteristics of a guided missile with an aircraft. The requirements called for a pilot, because the electro-mechanical guidance systems then under development for missiles were not progressing well.

Four companies responded with four designs: the Bachem BP20 *Natter* (Viper), Heinkel P.1077 *Julia*, Junkers EF127 *Walli*, and Messerschmitt P.1104. The development contract was awarded to Bachem, a newcomer and certainly no giant of industry. In its favor, the BP20 was a very simple and partly expendable design, made largely of wood, and fabricated in small components that could easily be handled by a dispersed, cottage industry, the short-term future for many German airframe builders.

The *Natter* was powered by a single liquid-propellant sustainer rocket engine, a Walter 109-509A-2 that was being used, and cursed, as the powerplant of Me163B interceptors. The BP20 was to be launched from a vertical rack by solid-propellant rocket boosters and aimed toward the bomb-

ers. Once within range, the pilot jettisoned a nose cap to expose a battery of two dozen 73 mm unguided *Föhn* rockets, then fired all in a single salvo. That done, he followed a complex ejection routine to bale out. He and the rocket engine were recovered by parachute; the rest of the *Natter* was expended.

Fifteen prototypes were built, the first tested in glides during October 1944. The first unpiloted booster-only vertical launch occurred December 22, and 10 followed in the test program. On February 23, 1945, a single unpiloted *Natter* was launched with boosters and sustainer operating. On the first piloted launch a few days later, the aircraft lost its canopy during the boost phase, rolled inverted, and slammed into the ground, killing the test pilot.

But the project continued in that strange limbo that persisted in early 1945 in Germany. The first 10 production *Natter*s were formed into an operational unit near the Wolf Hirth factory at Kirchheim but were destroyed before they saw action because of the advance of American ground forces. About 20 production *Natter*s had been built.

A mockup and two prototypes of Heinkel's P.1077 *Julia* and a single prototype of the Junkers EF127 *Walli* were under construction when troops overran their factories. Messerschmitt hadn't accomplished much more than a preliminary design of the P.1104 before the officers and designers were captured.

In August 1944, the Air Ministry circulated an Emergency Fighter Requirement to industry. The giants responded: Blohm und Voss submitted the tailless BV P.212, Heinkel the tailless P.1078C, and Junkers the tailless EF128. Messerschmitt proposed three different designs: P.1101, which later became a geometric prototype of the U.S. Bell X-5 research aircraft; the conventional P.1110; and the tailless P.1111. Focke-Wulf chief designer Kurt Tank submitted two versions of his Ta183, a podded fuselage with a horizontal tail set on an aft-swept vertical fin and rudder.

Focke-Wulf won that competition, and the Ta183-I

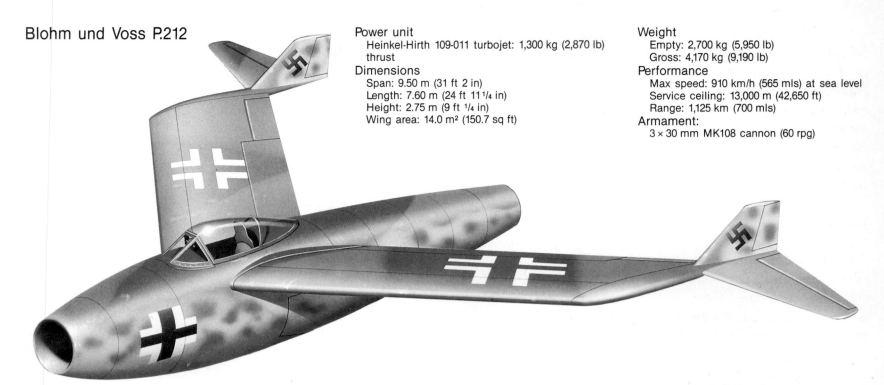

Blohm und Voss P.212

Power unit
Heinkel-Hirth 109-011 turbojet: 1,300 kg (2,870 lb) thrust
Dimensions
Span: 9.50 m (31 ft 2 in)
Length: 7.60 m (24 ft 11¼ in)
Height: 2.75 m (9 ft ¼ in)
Wing area: 14.0 m² (150.7 sq ft)

Weight
Empty: 2,700 kg (5,950 lb)
Gross: 4,170 kg (9,190 lb)
Performance
Max speed: 910 km/h (565 mls) at sea level
Service ceiling: 13,000 m (42,650 ft)
Range: 1,125 km (700 mls)
Armament:
3 × 30 mm MK108 cannon (60 rpg)

was ordered. By April, Focke-Wulf was in Allied territory and work had never gotten beyond the early design stages. (Tank later got to build at least one prototype, the *Pulqui* II, in Argentina.)

In September 1944, German industry was asked to develop a People's Fighter, simple and jet-propelled, with a minimum of strategic material in its structure. It would be flown, designers were told, by relatively inexperienced pilots. But there would be hundreds, even thousands of them, and they would overwhelm the bomber fleets. Arado, Blohm und Voss, Fieseler, Focke-Wulf, Heinkel, Junkers, and Messerschmitt proposed designs; Heinkel won with the He162, a single-jet design with the engine mounted centrally on the upper fuselage.

Heinkel performed a near-miracle. The company received a contract September 30, 1944, completed detail design October 29, and flew the first prototype December 6 (67 days, contract to first flight!). But even miracles could not meet the incredible production schedule: 1,000 a month by April 1945; 2,000 by May; 4,000 ultimately. Production was dispersed underground in mines, above-ground in factories. Amazingly, the first production aircraft were accepted in January 1945 and entered training programs the same month. One German pilot's logbook of his time in an He162 shows three flights in which he encountered enemy aircraft: Spitfire, Mosquito, and Typhoon. He claimed to have shot down the latter.

A day interceptor, powered by a ramjet engine, was the subject of requirements issued in October 1944. Dutifully, industry responded; paper studies were easy, and four were supplied: the Heinkel P.1080, Lippisch LP-13a (designed to burn powdered coal), Skoda-Kauba SK P.14, and Focke-Wulf Ta283. None went past the very preliminary design stage, although a few test programs for ramjet powerplants were under way late in the war.

In November 1944, a new program was started by the Air Ministry for a miniature fighter (*Miniaturjäger*). It was required to be mass-produced in quantity and to be deployed in masses to intercept bomber formations. The powerplant was a pulse-jet unit, as used on the infamous "Buzz-bomb." Its only saving graces were cheapness and relative simplicity. Industry responded with the Blohm und Voss P.213, Heinkel 162B, and

Junkers EF126 *Elli*, but other designers doubted the potential feasibility of the proposed aircraft. Junkers built a mockup, which was as far as any progressed.

At the end of November 1944, a high-level staff meeting in the Air Ministry confirmed the need for several of the last-ditch programs, based on their possible contribution to target defense. The staff decided to keep active, in order of priority, development of the Messerschmitt 262 with auxiliary rocket propulsion to improve its rate of climb; the Heinkel P.1077 *Julia*, then in prototype construction; the Junkers 248, an advanced version of the Me163B with longer endurance; and the Bachem BP20 *Natter*.

There was some dissent. The Heinkel *Julia* and the Bachem *Natter* were not very promising, it was stated, and both the *Julia* and *Walli* projects should be stopped. The only reason to continue the *Natter* was that it was nearly ready; but no production was planned. That decision, as was seen earlier, was not taken.

The rocket weapons research unit at Peenemünde had several missile projects in the works when the war ended, the most famous being the long-range A4 (V-2) ballistic missile. Its basic geometry, with low aspect-ratio wings added, was reproduced on a smaller scale in the *Wasserfall* (Waterfall) anti-aircraft missile, developed to carry a 235 kg (518 lb) warhead into the midst of a bomber formation. It would be able to loft that heavy explosive weight at twice the speed of sound to a maximum altitude of 20,000 m (65,600 ft). The first successful *Wasserfall* launch took place February 29, 1944, and the missile was scheduled to become operational with *Luftwaffe Flak* units in November 1945.

Five other rocket-powered anti-aircraft missiles were under development, and they were a cross-section of designers' dreams. Closest of all to operational use was the Henschel Hs117 *Schmetterling* (Butterfly), a subsonic weapon shaped like a small airplane. It was powered by a liquid-propellant rocket engine and was intended to make low- and medium-altitude intercepts, presumably against the devastating medium-bomber and fighter-bomber strikes. Test programs began in May 1944; production was ordered in December and began in March 1945 with a monthly target of 150 units. By November 1945, production facilities were expected to be turning out 3,000 a month.

The earliest of the German anti-aircraft missile programs was a venture by the Rheinmetall-Borsig company, producers of artillery and aircraft cannon and unguided rockets. Named *Rheintochter* (Daughter of the Rhein), it was an awkward-looking two-stage supersonic missile with steerable canard surfaces and six sweptback fins. The program began in November 1942, and a total of 82 test vehicles had been launched when it was abandoned in December 1944 because of its inability to reach bomber altitudes.

The *Taifun* (Typhoon) was an unguided rocket projectile to be fired in barrages from batteries of 12 launchers, each capable of firing 30 missiles in rapid succession. The plan called for deployment of 400 of these batteries to defend target areas, which would have required an initial consignment of 144,000 missiles. It was estimated that *Taifun* would become operational by September 1945, but the development site at Peenemünde was overrun by Russian troops in February 1945, and *Taifun* died in the ruins.

Messerschmitt proposed the *Enzian* (Gentian), a small pilotless aircraft looking much like the Me163B. It was designed to be boosted from a ramp by a pair of solid rockets, then climb at subsonic speed to the middle of a bomber formation, where it would detonate its 300 kg (661 lb) warhead and blow bombers all over the sky. The test program began in April 1944 and lasted through 38 test firings. *Enzian* was cancelled in January 1945, another casualty of inferior performance.

Rheinmetall-Borsig also developed an elegantly shaped anti-aircraft missile called *Feuerlilie* (Fire lily). It was tested and then cancelled in early 1945.

In the last months of the conflict, every company from Arado to Zeppelin proposed some specialized weapon, aircraft, or missile in an attempt to regain control of the air. Arado,

for example, proposed a tiny rocket interceptor of 5 m (16 ft 5 in) span. Focke-Wulf designed a vertical-takeoff rotary-winged fighter, with rotors propelled by ramjet engines. Zeppelin designed a rocket-powered interceptor and a rocket-powered ramming aircraft. None of these ideas moved beyond lines on paper.

Both the Japanese Army and Navy sponsored the development and, in some cases, ordered the production of a number of high-altitude fighters and interceptors to stem the B-29 tide. Most were conventional aircraft; many were derivatives of predecessor designs, and all were doomed by the inferior performance of available powerplants.

Kawasaki had a trio of Army projects under way at the end of the war. The Ki102A and Ki102C were twin-engined, two-seaters for high-altitude fighting and night interception respectively. Two Ki102C prototypes were destroyed before completion by the B-29s' air raids. Five of 25 completed Ki102As were delivered to the 28th *Hiko-Sentai* by May 1945 and were flown on several sorties before the war ended. The other Kawasaki project was the Ki108/Ki108-*Kai* high-altitude fighter, a single-seat, twin-engined aircraft with a pressurized cabin. Four prototypes were being tested as the war ended.

Mitsubishi had a pair of Army projects going. The Ki46-III-*Kai* was a modification of the well-known, respected reconnaissance aircraft the Allies called Dinah. A few of these twin-engined two-seaters became operational, but as fighters, their performance was not acceptable. The other Mitsubishi project was the Ki109, a four-place interceptor modified from the Ki67 heavy bomber and armed with a 75 mm Type 88 anti-aircraft gun. It was designed to counter the B-29s by climbing to high altitudes and firing from a great distance with its heavy-

Lippisch P.13a

Power unit
Lippisch coal-burning ramjet
Dimensions
Span: 5.92 m (19 ft 5 1/16 in)
Length: 6.70 m (21 ft 11 13/16 in)
Height: 3.18 m (10 ft 5 3/16 in)
Wing area: 20.0 m² (215.3 sq ft)
Weight
Gross: 2,300 kg (5,070 lb)
Performance
Max speed: 1,650 km/h (1,025 mls)
Endurance: 45 min on 800 kg (1,760 lb) coal fuel

Kyushu 18-*Shi* Interceptor *Shinden* (J7W1)

Power unit
  Mitsubish Ha 43-42 18-cylinder air-cooled engine:
  2,030 hp for take-off
  1,600 hp at 8,400 m (27,560 ft)
Dimensions
  Span: 11.14 m (36 ft 5 9/16 in)
  Length, level position: 9.76 m (32 ft 1/4 in)
  Height, on the ground, over canopy: 3.555 m (11 ft 8 in)
  Wing area: 20.5 m² (220.7 sq ft)

Weights
  Empty: 3,465 kg (7,639 lb)
  Gross: 4,928 kg (10,864 lb)

Performance (production type, planned)
  Max speed: 741 km/h (460 mph) at 8,700 m (28,540 ft)
  Time to climb to 8,000 m (26,250 ft): 10 min 40 sec
  Service ceiling: 12,000 m (39,370 ft)
Armament
  4 × 30 mm Type 5 Mk 1-B cannon (60 rpg)

caliber weapon. By the time the airplane was developed and 22 had been produced, the B-29s had changed tactics to low-level night raids. The Ki109s became hangar queens.

Nakajima built one Ki87, a turbo-supercharged single-seat fighter, test-flown in April 1945, which never reached production. Tachikawa's Ki94-I was an unusual attempt to build a twin-engined, single-seat high-altitude fighter, with engines mounted in front of and behind the cockpit. The project was cancelled, and an orthodox single-engined Ki94-II with a pressurized cabin was developed. It was scheduled to fly August 18, 1945.

The Navy Aichi S1A *Denko* was a projected radar-equipped twin-engined, two-seat night fighter. Two prototypes were begun, but both were incomplete when they were destroyed by bombing raids. A similar fate befell the Kawanishi N1K5-J prototype, a modified N1K2-J (George) fighter. Designed to intercept B-29s, it was destroyed in its hangar by a B-29's bombs.

The Kyushu J7W *Shinden*, one of the war's three canard designs, was planned as a high-altitude interceptor. A single example was built and flown three times—August 3, 6, and 8, 1945—only days before the war ended.

Mitsubishi had two Navy fighter/interceptor projects in development at the end of the war. The A7M3-J *Reppu-Kai* was a single-seat, single-engined fighter which proceeded no

further than a mockup. Second was the J8M *Shusui*, inspired by the Messerschmitt Me163B. Production was established, five had been built, and one test flight made on July 7, 1945. The J8M crashed on that flight, killing the test pilot.

Last of the Navy projects was Nakajima's J5N1 *Tenrai*, a single-seat, twin-engined interceptor. Six prototypes were built, and the first prototype flew as early as July 1944, but the type was never ordered into production.

Many have extrapolated beyond these projects, speculating what might have happened had any of them become operational in quantity six months or a year earlier. But unusual designs are not enough to win a war. If, for example, Germany had been earlier with the Messerschmitt 262, the *Luftwaffe*'s requirements for fuel supplies and transportation would have increased tremendously. Early jet engines were very thirsty and burned about a pound (0.45 kg) of fuel each second for every pound of thrust they generated. In a similar fashion, a full-scale offensive with rocket weapons would have required several times the output of the entire European production of liquid oxygen.

And where would the pilots have come from? By 1943, the decreasing quality of the average German and Japanese pilots was obvious to Allied bomber and fighter pilots. Even suicide tactics—assumed at high levels to require less piloting skill and training—would have required pilots who knew enough about flying to get off the ground without crashing; who could navigate, or at least follow a flight leader; and who could hit a moving target in a dive from high altitude, assuming they got through the anti-aircraft and fighter defenses. Suicide tactics were terribly successful against ships anchored off Okinawa. But that was at once the beginning and the end of any such tactic in strength.

Speculation is always interesting, and these paragraphs of pessimism may be as wrong as those written to predict a German or a Japanese victory, "if only..." One thing is certain. The tactics of interceptors against heavy bombers originated earlier than World War II and have persisted later. But they were at their absolute zenith in those years between September 1939 and August 1945, between *Blitzkrieg* and A-bomb. These words are intended to recognize an exceptional phase of war in the air, which we will not likely see again.

A Ki87 high-altitude experimental fighter completed at Nakajima's Mitaka factory, Tokyo in February 1945. (Yoji Watanabe)

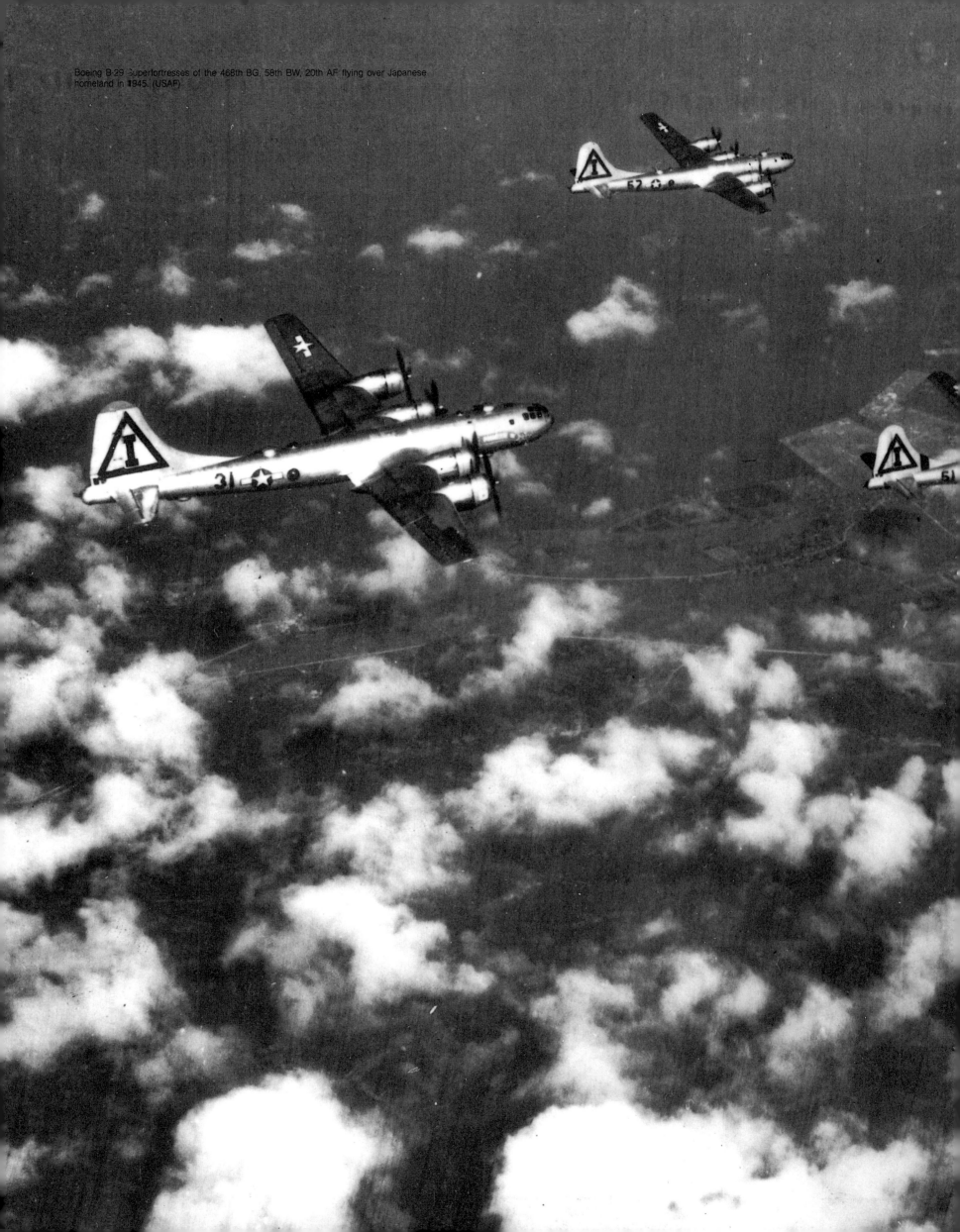

Boeing B-29 Superfortresses of the 468th BG, 58th BW, 20th AF flying over Japanese homeland in 1945. (USAF)